Sociological Beginnings

STUDIES IN SOCIAL AND POLITICAL THOUGHT 11

STUDIES IN SOCIAL AND POLITICAL THOUGHT
Editor: Gerard Delanty, *University of Liverpool*

This series publishes peer-reviewed scholarly books on all aspects of
social and political thought. It will be of interest to scholars and
advanced students working in the areas of social theory and sociology,
the history of ideas, philosophy, political and legal theory, anthropological and cultural theory. Works of individual scholarship will have
preference for inclusion in the series, but appropriate co- or multi-
authored works and edited volumes of outstanding quality or
exceptional merit will also be included. The series will also consider
English translations of major works in other languages.

Challenging and intellectually innovative books are particularly
welcome on the history of social and political theory; modernity and the
social and human sciences; major historical or contemporary thinkers;
the philosophy of the social sciences; theoretical issues on the transformation of contemporary society; social change and European
societies.

It is not series policy to publish textbooks, research reports,
empirical case studies, conference proceedings or books of an essayist
or polemical nature.

Sociological Beginnings

The First Conference of the

German Society for Sociology

CHRISTOPHER ADAIR-TOTEFF

LIVERPOOL UNIVERSITY PRESS

First published 2005 by
Liverpool University Press
4 Cambridge Street
Liverpool
L69 7ZU

British Library Cataloguing-in-Publication Data
A British Library CIP Record is available

ISBN 0–85323–799-9 cased
　　　0–85323–809-X limp

Typeset in Plantin by Koinonia, Bury
Printed and bound in the European Union by Bell & Bain Ltd, Glasgow

Für mein Schatz

Contents

Preface

Sociology has been a part of academic programmes for so long that it is difficult to imagine a time when not only was it not recognized as a discipline but it did not really even exist. Today, the names Max Weber, Ferdinand Tönnies, Georg Simmel and Ernst Troeltsch are familiar to most sociologists. However, none of these was an academic or professional sociologist, because neither of those classifications existed during their formative years, before 1890. The first sociology professorship in Germany began in 1918, the year that Simmel died. Weber's death occurred two years later; and Troeltsch died in 1923. Only Tönnies lived long enough to see sociology become an academic and professional discipline.

Simmel and Tönnies read philosophy, Weber was educated as a lawyer and Troeltsch was trained as a theologian. Yet these four thinkers were instrumental in fostering sociology in Germany. Specifically, Tönnies, Simmel, and Weber helped form the Deutsche Gesellschaft für Soziologie (D.G.S.) (German Society for Sociology) in 1909. A year later, they, along with Troeltsch, Sombart and a few others took part in the first sociology conference in Germany. They arranged to have their papers published with the discussions that followed some of the lectures, and their publication appeared in 1911. Five of the nine papers are translated here in their entirety; and I present synopses of the others with some of the discussions that followed. The five major papers cover a wide range of issues, including natural law, journalism and technology, but all treat the topics from a sociological standpoint. Three can be considered to focus mostly on substantial issues, whereas two are primarily methodological in scope.

None of the five thinkers (Weber, Simmel, Tönnies, Troeltsch, or Sombart) founded any 'school' and all five fell out of favour. However, there has been a

Preface

resurgence of interest in Weber and Simmel for several decades, and for Tönnies and Troeltsch for close to 15 years. Because of his later writings, Sombart has been dismissed as a Nazi sympathizer, but regardless of the merits of this charge, we should not be blind to the greatness of his earlier work, especially his work on the origins of capitalism. All five were interested in historical matters, but not simply for history's sake. All were preoccupied with the problems of modernity and the five papers they presented display this concern in varying degrees. Because they came from different educational disciplines, all were able to diagnose the various problems of modernity – and for all of them, this meant sociological problems. All sought solutions to the socio-economic, political and even religious problems of the day, but all of them also recognized the importance of keeping their scholarly research free from their ideological agendas. Weber adhered most strongly to this belief, but it was also true of Troeltsch and Tönnies, if less so for Simmel and Sombart. We need to remind ourselves that they, like us, lived in uncertain times. Those times were also marred by wars and revolutions and by economic and political collapses. These thinkers looked to the past to try to understand the present and perhaps even predict a sense of the future. They all repudiated grandiose theories but they were also wary of meaningless data. As Neo-Kantians, they subscribed to a form of Kant's *Mittelweg* – his 'middle way' between the English empiricism embodied by Newton and the German idealism championed by Leibniz. For Weber and the other four, the 'middle way' was their belief in empirical research, coupled with conceptual ideals.

The idea of this book grew out of the recognition that in their papers, these five thinkers were offering new and important ideas in a new and important context. All had established themselves as first-rate thinkers, but all were considered intellectual 'outsiders'. Weber and Troeltsch were fortunate to be appointed to professorships at a relatively early age, but because of their real or imagined socialist inclinations, the three others were forced to wait for decades. That all were 'outsiders' is easy to understand, given that all five rejected contemporary academic classifications, and that they disdained traditional 'academic turf wars' and instead sought to develop a new 'science' that would bring together new ways of looking at old and new problems. Because of this, I began to concentrate much of my research first on Simmel and Tönnies, then on Troeltsch and Weber. My work concentrated primarily on their better-known works, such as Simmel's *Soziologie*, Tönnies' *Gemeinschaft und Gesellschaft*, and Weber's *Wirtschaft und Gesellschaft*. But I became convinced that these five papers were undeservedly neglected, in German and even more so in English. They show these thinkers at the height of their powers, engaged in critical discussions about questions of the day – questions that are still pertinent today. Hence, I deemed it important to offer translations of these papers in order to bring more attention to them, especially for the English-speaking audience. Because these papers were presented at the birth of German sociology, I thought it might be fitting to call this book *Sociological Beginnings*.

I owe at least two debts of gratitude. First, I wish to thank Stephen Turner for his continual encouragement over the past decade and a half and particularly for his insistence that I show the importance and relevance of Neo-Kantianism in many of its forms. Second, I want to thank my wife, Stephanie Adair-Toteff, for her encouragement of all my work, but especially this one. I spell out my thanks in the Note on Translation, but I want to acknowledge my overall debt of gratitude to her here. I could not have done this book without her help. For what is right in this book she is at least partially responsible; what is wrong is still fully my fault. I hope that this book will prompt scholars and students to look more carefully at the smaller and less well known works of these thinkers. And when we have a full understanding of these thinkers, we may also have a better understanding of ourselves.

Pfingsten/Whit Sunday, 2005
Übersee am Chiemsee, Oberbayern

A Note on Translation

Every translator has to find the safest passage between the Scylla of being too literal and the Charybdis of being too figurative. Simmel, Tönnies, Weber, Troeltsch and, to a lesser extent, Sombart, offer immense challenges to the translator. Not only does one need to make that decision about literalness but one must also decide what to do about translating certain sentences and certain words. To offer a few examples: one of Simmel's sentences runs to 13 lines, has 7 commas, 3 colons, 1 semi-colon and 1 question mark. This single sentence contains some 120 words. It includes the terms *Läppischkeit* and *Reibungswiderstände*, both of which resist translation. The first is close to 'childlike' or 'nonsense', but 'foolishness' is what I chose. The second is a compound formed by joining *Reibungs* and *Widestände*. *Reibung'* is 'rubbing' or 'friction' and *Widerstände* are 'resistances', so I offer the somewhat accurate but unwieldly 'friction resistances'. Tönnies is not much easier: he has one sentence that takes 14 lines, contains 120 words, and has 13 commas, 2 semi-colons and 1 colon. Troeltsch is for the most part better, but many of his sentences have several clauses, so that one is not always certain about what refers to what. Even when his sentences are relatively straightforward, his expectation that his audience has more than a passing familiarity with major and minor figures in philosophy, theology and even jurisprudence is an expectation that was probably too high in 1910 and is certainly beyond many educated people today. This is not a problem in translation, but it is a problem for the translator. Rather than weigh down every page with translator's notes and clarifications, I have tried to offer them only when I believed them absolutely necessary. As for Weber, we have it on Karl Jaspers' authority that Weber was unconcerned about style. Of the five, Sombart, is (relatively) easier to translate because he tends to write in (relatively) short sentences. But his arguments are often vague and sometimes seemingly contradictory. Sombart did care about style, but in places he sounds simply bombastic. He likes to employ exclamation marks after single words (*Wissenschaft!*), several words (*Die Kunst!*), and after sentences: (*Werfen wir sodann einen Blick auf geistige Kultur!*). But many of these words are difficult to translate. *Wissenschaft* is often rendered as 'science', but in German it has a wider meaning, something closer to 'knowledge'; and *geistige* is somewhere between 'mental' and 'spiritual'.

I would like to believe that I am in a fairly good position to be able to convey the points of these papers to the reader. Being trained as a philosopher and a historian of philosophy has helped me considerably. More importantly, I have been concerned with Neo-Kantianism for more than a decade. Having focused on Simmel, Tönnies, Troeltsch and Weber, I think I have a good grasp of the essence of their thinking. But for translating, I have relied on my wife Stephanie's expertise more times than I care to count. Being a native-born German, truly bilingual, as well as a sociologist, she has shed considerable light on the untangling of some of their sentences. Our efforts seem to underscore one of the central points of her dissertation from twenty years ago: linguistics is often a matter of relativity. It goes without saying that despite her help I have made mistakes and that I am solely responsible for all of them.

Many people have insisted that translating is a thankless task. If I have succeeded in conveying the thoughts of these great scholars, I have thanks enough.

Chronology

1908 Simmel's *Soziologie* is published
1909 Deutsche Gesellschaft für Soziologie (D.G.S.) is founded in Berlin
1910 First conference of D.G.S. is held in Frankfurt
1912 Troeltsch's *Soziallehren* is published in its completed form. Second conference of the D.G.S. is held in Berlin. Weber withdraws from the D.G.S.
1913 Sombart's *Bourgeois* is published. Tönnies is finally appointed professor at Kiel
1914 The First World War begins. Deaths of Heidelberg professors Wilhelm Windelband and Emil Lask. Simmel rejected at Heidelberg but receives Chair at Strasbourg
1915 Sinking of the Lusitania. Weber warns of increased U-boat warfare. Troeltsch moves to Berlin
1917 The USA enters the war. Weber presents *Wissenschaft als Beruf*
1918 First World War ends. Revolutions in Russia. First Chair in Sociology at Frankfurt. Simmel dies
1919 Revolutions in Germany. Weber accepts Chair in Munich. Weber presents *Politik als Beruf*
1920 Weber dies. Weber's *Religionssoziologie* is published in book form
1921 Weber's *Wirtschaft und Gesellschaft* and *Gesammelte Politische Schriften* are published. Massive inflation in Germany
1922 Third conference of D.G.S. is held in Jena. Troeltsch's *Der Historismus und seine Probleme* is published
1923 Troeltsch dies
1924 Fourth conference of D.G.S. is held in Heidelberg
1926 Fifth conference of D.G.S. is held in Vienna
1927 Heidegger's *Sein und Zeit* is published
1928 Sixth conference of D.G.S. is held in Zurich
1930 Seventh conference of D.G.S. is held in Berlin
1933 Hitler becomes Chancellor of Germany. Tönnies is forced to retire
1936 Tönnies dies
1939 Second World War begins
1941 Sombart dies

Short Biographies of the Main Participants of the First D.G.S. Conference

Buber, Martin (8 February 1878–13 June 1965). Philosopher of Religion. From 1924 until 1933 he was Professor of Philosophy at Frankfurt. In 1938 he left for Palestine, where he was Professor of the Sociology of Religion at the Hebrew University. His most important book was *Ich und Du* (*I and Thou*) (1922). He was editor of a number of influential journals and of the critical series *Die Gesellschaft* (*Society*), which included books by Simmel, Tönnies and Sombart and also by Willy Hellpach, Gustav Landauer and Eduard Bernstein.

Gothein, Eberhard (29 October 1853–13 November 1923). Political economist and cultural historian. Received his doctorate in 1877 in Breslau and gained his 'Habilitation'[1] there in 1879. In 1904 he became Weber's successor at Heidelberg, where he remained until 1923. Weber expressly appreciated his *Wirtschaftsgeschichte Schwarzwalds* (*Economic History of the Black Forest*) (1892). He was a contributor to Weber's *Grundriß der Sozilökonomik*.

Kantorowicz, Hermann (18 November 1877–12 February 1940). Legal historian. Received his doctorate in jurisprudence in 1900 at Heidelberg and gained his 'Habilitation' in Freiburg in 1908. He was a professor there until 1927, when he became visiting professor at Columbia University, USA. From 1929 until 1933, when he was dismissed on racial grounds, he was professor at Kiel. He emigrated to the USA.

Michels, Robert (1 January 1876–3 May 1936). German–Italian social scientist. Received his doctorate in 1900 at Halle, but because of his socialist leanings he was unable to work towards his 'Habilitation' in Germany and

---

1 *Habilitationsschrift* is the post-doctoral thesis or other work necessary in Germany and other European countries for a university teaching post.

eventually gained it in 1907 in Turin. From 1914 until 1928 was an ordinary professor at Basel, and from 1928 until 1933 at Perugia. He dedicated his *Soziologie des Parteiwesens* (*Sociology of Parties*) (1911) to Max Weber. Weber distanced himself from Michels in 1915 because of Michel's accusations about Germany's war position. He was a contributor to Weber's *Grundriß der Sozialökonomik*.

Ploetz, Alfred (22 August 1860–20 March 1940). A doctor of medicine and a leading proponent of Racial Biology. Received his medical degree in 1890 at Zurich and went into private practice.

Schulze-Gaevernitz, Gerhart von (25 July 1864–10 July 1943). Political economist. Received his doctorate in jurisprudence in 1886 at Göttingen and achieved his 'Habilitation' in 1891 at Leipzig. From 1896–1923 he was ordinary professor at Freiburg, and was friendly with Weber from their Freiburg days. He contributed to Weber's *Grundriß der Sozialökonomik*.

Simmel, Georg (1 March 1858–26 September 1918). Philosopher and sociologist. Received his doctorate in philosophy in 1881 at Berlin and was promoted there in 1885. Was extraordinary professor at Berlin from 1901 until 1914, when he became ordinary professor at Strasbourg. He and his wife Getrud were close friends of the Webers from the late 1890s.

Sombart, Werner (19 January 1863–18 May 1941). Political economist. Received his doctorate in philosophy in 1888 at Berlin. He was extraordinary professor at Breslau from 1890 until 1906; ordinary professor at the Handelhochschule in Berlin from 1906; and ordinary professor at Berlin from 1917 until 1931. He was Co-Editor of the *Archiv für Sozialwissenschaft und Sozialpolitik* with Max Weber and Edgar Jaffé and was on friendly terms with Max Weber until the First World War.

Tönnies, Ferdinand (26 July 1855–9 April 1936). Philosopher and sociologist. Received his doctorate in philosophy in 1877 at Tübingen and, in 1881, gained his 'Habilitation' at Kiel. He was extraordinary professor there from 1909 and ordinary professor from 1913 until 1933.

Troeltsch, Ernst (17 February 1865–1 February 1923). Theologian and philosopher. Received his doctorate in theology in 1891 at Göttingen and received his 'Habilitation' there during the same year. From 1893 he was ordinary professor at Heidelberg and from 1915–23 at Berlin. He was close to Max Weber from 1900 until 1915; between 1910 and 1915 he and his wife Marta lived in the top floor of Weber's Heidelberg residence.

Main Participants in the First D.G.S. Conference

Voigt, Andreas (18 April 1860–10 January 1941). Political economist. Received his doctorate in 1890 at Freiburg. He was ordinary professor of political economy at Frankfurt.

Weber, Max (21 April 1864–14 June 1920). Political economist and sociologist. Received his doctorate in law in 1889 at Berlin and his 'Habilitation' there in 1891. He was Professor of Political Economy at Freiburg from 1893 until 1896 and Professor of Economics at Heidelberg from 1897 until 1903. He experienced periods of mental illness between 1897 and 1903, when he retired from Heidelberg. He was Co-Editor of the *Archiv für Sozialwissenschaft und Sozialpolitik* with Edgar Jaffé and Werner Sombart and Editor of the *Grundriß der Sozialökonomik*.

Introduction

Today, sociology and sociologists are accepted – and even respected – worldwide. Sociology has long been regarded as a legitimate science. Most universities have a sociology department; there are numerous sociology journals; and sociology conferences are held regularly. The 2002 World Congress of the International Association of Sociology brought together thousands of sociologists from 100 different countries. Besides the International Sociological Association, there are the British Sociological Association, the American Sociology Association and the Deutsche Gesellschaft für Soziologie (D.G.S.).

By contrast with today, sociology as a science barely existed 100 years ago (Hawthorne, 2004: 245). While Auguste Comte may have coined the term 'sociology' early in the nineteenth century, the science of sociology was still in its infancy in 1900. Five years earlier, Emile Durkheim had published *Les Règles de la Méthode Sociologique* and by 1905 Albion Small had established the so-called Chicago school.[1] But in Germany, there were still no professional sociologists or professional sociological associations, no sociological journals and no academic sociological conferences. This began to change in 1909. As Dirk Käsler has argued, for sociology to succeed in Germany, it needed to become institutionalized, and this began when the Deutsche Gesellschaft für Soziologie was founded in Berlin on 3 January of that year (Käsler, 1984: 294). Not only did it need to become institutionalized, it also needed to be regarded as non-partisan and objective. It had to dissociate itself from the idealistic and socialist-leaning socio-political movements of the day. Sociology did not arise in Germany as Athena sprang out of Zeus's head; rather, there was a long gestation period.

1 It is worth noting that Small had a considerable interest in Simmel's writings and began translating some of Simmel's works around 1896 (Frisby, 1991: 237).

1

Sociological Beginnings

In his 'Die Anfänge der Soziologie' ('The Beginnings of Sociology') Werner Sombart discussed this gestation period. He traced the beginnings of sociology in general to the time when neither natural law theories nor contract theories of law held sway. According to Sombart, only when there was no 'absolute' could a science of 'sociology' become possible (Sombart, 1923: 9). Thus, for Sombart, sociology 'began' some time in the last decades of the eighteenth century. As to the question of when German sociology 'began', there can be a more definite answer: 1887. That was the year Ferdinand Tönnies published his highly influential book *Gemeinschaft und Gesellschaft* (*Community and Society*) (see Käsler, 1984: 305). It was, as Jose Harris has suggested, 'a work of precocious immaturity' (Tönnies, 2001: xv) and at first it did not receive much attention. But by the turn of the century it began to command attention, in part because Tönnies' book fitted rather well with other Neo-Kantian philosophical works dealing with cultural problems. In order to understand this, it is helpful briefly to set out who the Neo-Kantians were and how they were indebted to Kant's work and built upon it.

In the *Kritik der reinen Vernunft* (*Critique of Pure Reason*) Immanuel Kant tried to set out the origins and limits of knowledge. He traced these back to two 'faculties' of the mind – 'sensibility' and 'understanding'. Both were formal, or pure, meaning that they were a priori to experience, but provided the conditions that made experience possible. The a priori aspect of the faculty of 'sensibility' guaranteed the universality and necessity of Euclidean geometry; while the a priori aspect of the faculty of 'understanding' guaranteed the validity and applicability of Newtonian science. In particular, Kant demonstrated that the necessary validity of 'causality' is founded upon the selection processes of the mind rather than simply being 'given' to us, along with a multiplicity of other things. As Kant maintained, what is 'given' to us is the mere play of things; the workings of our minds impose order and regularity, i.e. experience.

Kant's gift was to show that the mind's a priori selection processes guarantee the universality and necessity of mathematics and of natural science. And many of Kant's followers were content to offer minor improvements on Kant's philosophy. But what many of the Neo-Kantians hoped to do was to understand Kant better.[2] For Hermann Cohen and Paul Natorp, this meant publishing commentaries and works showing not only what Kant *meant* but also what Kant *should have meant*. Other Neo-Kantians wanted to use Kantian methodology to expand the range of subjects and to show that there could be sciences of them. Georg Simmel tried to establish a reputable philosophy of history; and Heinrich Rickert tried to do the same for culture. Most notably,

2 For a long account of Neo-Kantianism, see Willey, 1978; and for a shorter one see Adair-Toteff, 2003.

Rickert, Weber's friend and colleague, published both parts of *Die Grenzen der naturwissenschaftlichen Begriffsbildung* (*The Limits of Concept Formation in the Natural Sciences*) in 1902. In this work, Rickert sought to show how the natural sciences developed general laws, whereas the historical sciences needed to develop methods to allow for knowledge of history and culture. Using a similar Kantian process of selection, Rickert attempted to expand Kantian methodology to also cover history and culture. In the smaller version of his work, which he called *Kulturwissenschaft und Naturwissenschaft* (*Cultural Science and Natural Science*) (1899), Rickert emphasized that his interest was primarily in culture rather than in history. In this, he was continuing the Neo-Kantian investigations into the world of cultural experience.

The notion of culture also played a central role in the journal *Logos*. The subtitle was *Internationale Zeitschrift für Philosophie der Kultur* (*International Journal for the Philosophy of Culture*). Rickert was a major contributor to this remarkable journal, beginning with the first issue, of 1910/1911. This issue included works by Henri Bergson, Benedetto Croce and Edmund Husserl, in addition to Georg Simmel and Ernst Troeltsch.[3]

Troeltsch was also a contributor to another important and highly influential journal – the *Archiv für Sozialwissenschaft und Sozialpolitik* (*Archive for Social Science and Social Politics*) edited by Max Weber, Werner Sombart and Edgar Jaffé. They took over the editorship in 1904 and made it a priority to publish only non-partisan, scholarly works. Weber made this intention abundantly clear in his introductory essay, 'Die "Objektivität" sozialwissenschaftlicher und sozialpolitischer Erkenntnis' ('The "Objectivity" of Social Scientific and Social Policy Knowledge') (Weber, 1922a: 147–48). The journal was reserved for those who wanted to further scientific understanding; those wishing to pursue partisan politics were strongly urged to look elsewhere.

Weber published his *Protestantische Ethik und der Geist des Kapitalismus* (*Protestant Ethic and the Spirit of Capitalism*) in the journal in two instalments in 1904 and 1905; and he arranged to publish Troeltsch's *Soziallehren der christlichen Kirchen und Gruppen* (*Social Teachings of the Christian Churches*), which appeared in instalments from 1908 to 1910. Sombart, Tönnies and Robert Michels published a number of articles in the *Archiv*.

Whereas *Logos* was devoted to the philosophy of culture and the *Archiv* focused on socio-political questions, the *Gesellschaft* (*Society*) series of small books dealt with questions relating to contemporary society. This important series was produced under the editorship of Martin Buber, who would later

---

3 The series ran until 1932. Other contributors included Georg Lukacs, Nikolai Hartmann, Paul Natorp, Ernst Cassirer, Hans Kelsen, Hans-Georg Gadamer, Paul Tillich, Karl Löwith, Rudolf Otto, Hermann Kantorowicz and Max and Marianne Weber.

make a name for himself as the author of *Ich and Du* (*I and Thou*) and a reputation as an existentialist writer. But this series, which ran from 1905–1909, dealt with more specific issues. As Buber put it in his introduction to the series, its intention was to focus on the problems of reality in a socio-psychological manner (see Sombart, 1905: IX–XIII).

The first volume to appear was Sombart's *Das Proletariat*. Sombart had earned a name for himself with his research into the origins of modern capitalism (Sombart, 1902) but much of his work also dealt with socialist issues. Just as Marx had publicized the tragic aspects of capitalism, Sombart did much the same in *Das Proletariat*. He discussed in considerable detail the appalling working and living conditions of German workers and their families (Sombart, 1905: 25–32). Especially disturbing were his accounts of the working lives of women and children (Sombart, 1905: 41–55, 71–75).

Sombart's book was followed the next year by Eduard Bernstein's *Der Streik* (*The Strike*). Like Sombart, Bernstein attempted to provide an analysis of the essence and the effects of capitalism, in this case in the discussion of one of the few tools left to the worker – the strike (Bernstein, 1906: 23–25, 65). For Bernstein, this was a matter of war (Bernstein: 1906: 49, 79). More specifically, it was a matter of revolution. That was the focus of Gustav Landauer's 1907 contribution of the same name. Much of Landauer's book was historical rather than sociological in nature and he made some rather startling claims. He insisted that sociology is no science and that the 'form' of the Middle Ages was not the state but was 'society' (Landauer, 1907: 7, 46). But he offered a penetrating socio-political analysis of revolution. He pointed out that the occurrence of revolutions cannot be predicted; that while taking place, they have a dream or nightmare quality; and that their outcome is often not what was wanted or expected (Landauer, 1907: 81–83, 92–93, 119). And he insisted that 'society is older than the individual' (Landauer, 1907: 48).

For Simmel, society necessarily involved exchange, if not conflict. In *Die Religion* (*Religion*), Simmel opined that while there may be equality before God, the differences in interests, purposes and drives help determine various social interactions (Simmel, 1905: 81, 24). In Simmel's delineation of *Gesellschaft* there are conflicting interactions, a point with which Tönnies concurred in his *Die Sitte* (*Morals*, or *Customs*) (Tönnies, 1909). In *Gemeinschaft und Gesellschaft* Tönnies had argued that there are a number of oppositions, the most important being the opposition between *Gemeinschaft* and *Gesellschaft*. For Tönnies, *Gesellschaft* was artificial and mechanical, whereas *Gemeinschaft* was natural and organic – in the first, people were isolated; whereas in the second, they were connected (Tönnies, 1991: 3, 34, 20; see Adair-Toteff, 1995: 60–61). Tönnies preferred *Gemeinschaft* to *Gesellschaft* because of the naturalness and the interconnectedness, but also, as he argued in *Die Sitte*, because it represented *Das Volk* ('the people'), and only where there is *Gemeinschaft* can 'customary morality' be found (Tönnies, 1909: 14, 59). Tönnies' preference for *Gemeinschaft* did not blind him to the 'inevitability' of *Gesellschaft* and he dedicated much of his life to the founding of an independent and academically respectable science of society – sociology.

The Five Main Speakers:
Simmel, Tönnies, Weber, Sombart and Troeltsch

The interconnections of the Neo-Kantians offer a fascinating insight into the world of German academe, but the relations between Simmel, Tönnies, Weber, Sombart, and Troeltsch are particularly interesting. From a variety of sources, including books, articles and letters, we learn that their relationships were often complex. Sometimes they were in agreement, as when Weber and Troeltsch defended each other from rather ill-considered attacks on their treatments of Protestant capitalism. And Weber expressly relied on certain writings of Simmel, Sombart, Tönnies and Troeltsch. Yet although Troeltsch greatly admired Simmel's thinking, he believed him mistaken on a number of matters, ranging from history to religion. And Sombart took issue with Weber's Protestant sources of capitalism while Weber thought that Sombart's books were often not well argued. Tönnies was often at odds with Weber and Troeltsch and, unlike Simmel, he concentrated on sociological industrial concerns. Even though they got into heated arguments – Weber broke off relations briefly with Tönnies and for longer with Troeltsch – they stood together in their attempts to make the various studies of societies respectable. This meant broadening the recognition of sociology and showing that its focus was on facts and not on values. In what follows, I try to provide a short biographical sketch of each of the five, showing how they were ideally suited to start the D.G.S. At first glance, Tönnies' background and interests may not have suggested this.

Ferdinand Tönnies

Tönnies was born on 26 July 1855 in the rural area outside Husum in Schleswig-Holstein, in what is now northern Germany. Like many German students, he attended a number of universities. He studied at Jena, Leipzig, Bonn and Berlin before settling on Tübingen. There, he continued the philo-sophical studies he had begun in Berlin with the noted Neo-Kantian, Friedrich Paulsen. He received his doctorate in philosophy (actually on Greek philology) in 1877. One of Tönnies' early philosophical interests was Nietzsche. In his autobiographical sketch, he recounts how he was fascinated by Nietzsche's early works, revelling in some of them and feeling as if they were revelations (Tönnies, 1922: 5–7). However, Tönnies came to reject Nietzsche, especially the later works. In particular, he warned of the 'fire water' contained in *Also Sprach Zarathustra* (*Thus Spake Zarathustra*) (Tönnies, 1892: 1612–13). Tönnies continued his critique of Nietzsche and his adherents in *Der Nietzsche-Kultus. Eine Kritik* (*The Nietzsche Cult. A Critique*). Simmel reviewed Tönnies' book and he hints at the reason why Tönnies came to reject Nietzsche. As a modern socialist, Tönnies disapproved of Nietzsche's elitist tendencies (Simmel, 1897: 1646). Yet he also objected to the misunderstanding and misuse of Nietzsche's thinking by the masses.

Another of Tönnies' main philosophical interests was Thomas Hobbes. This study resulted in *Hobbes. Leben und Lehre* (*Hobbes. Life and Teaching*), which was published in 1896. It grew out of a number of papers that Tönnies had published from 1879 to 1881. Tönnies concentrated more on social and socialist philosophy, however, and that meant working on Karl Marx. Marx was important for *Gemeinschaft und Gesellschaft*, but Tönnies did not publish his major work on Marx until 1923. Like Sombart, he was interested in the rise of socialism in many parts of Europe. In his *Die Entwicklung der sozialen Frage* (*The Development of the Social Question*) Tönnies discussed the origin and rise of socialism in Great Britain, France and Germany (Tönnies, 1907: 24–136). He would continue to maintain an interest in Britain, but his primary focus was always on Germany. This is evident in the work for which he is most famous: *Gemeinschaft und Gesellschaft* (*Community and Society*) (1887).

The first reactions to *Gemeinschaft und Gesellschaft* were not universally positive. Durkheim disapproved of Tönnies' one-sided endorsement of *Gemeinschaft*.[4] Weber thought highly of the book, calling it 'the beautiful work' (Weber, 1922b: 1). By the second edition of 1912, the reception was large and appreciative. Sociology was also becoming more respectable, so Tönnies' change to the subtitle may have been more an appreciation of sociology than a repudiation of socialism. The original subtitle was: *Abhandlung des Communismus und des Socialismus als empirischer Culturformen* (*Treatise on Communism and Socialism as Empirical Cultural Forms*); it now became: *Grundbegriff der reinen Soziologie* (*Fundamental Concepts of Pure Sociology*). Further works on sociology appeared, including *Soziologische Studien und Kritiken* (*Sociological Studies and Critiques*), which was published between 1925 and 1929 in three volumes; and

4 Liebersohn, 1988: 11–12. Gerd Schroeter claimed that in the first 25 years, only 750 copies were sold, but the second edition began to change that. After the First World War, it had become 'a bestseller' (Schroeter, 1993: 60).

Einführung in die Soziologie (*Introduction to Sociology*), published in 1931. By 1935, *Gemeinschaft und Gesellschaft* had gone through eight editions.

Tönnies' early publishing successes did not translate into academic success. He began teaching at the University of Kiel in 1881. However, partly because of his socialist tendencies, partly because of his help for striking dockers and partly because of his independent thinking, Tönnies was not appointed to a professorship until 1913. By then, it was virtually impossible for the political and academic authorities not to offer him a professorship. He continued to teach at Kiel. In 1932, Tönnies advocated resisting fascism, and in 1933 the local Nazis stripped him of his honorary professorship, his pension and his personal library. As early as 1922 Tönnies had insisted that 'Force is not authority' (Tönnies, 1922: 33). He died on 9 April 1936.

Georg Simmel

Like Tönnies, Georg Simmel suffered academic difficulties. But unlike Tönnies, Simmel grew up in cosmopolitan Berlin. He was born there on 1 March 1858 and received his doctorate in philosophy from Berlin University in 1881. His dissertation, on Kant's science, was followed by a number of short works on psychology. In 1892, Simmel published two major works: *Die Probleme der Geschichtsphilosophie* (*The Problems of the Philosophy of History*) and the massive, two-volume *Einleitung in die Moralwissenschaft* (*Introduction to Moral Science*). Like Tönnies, Simmel had little luck in getting promoted to a regular professorship; and he also feared that he would be an 'eternal *Privatdozent*' [unsalaried lecturer] (Tönnies, 1922: 22). As Werner Jung put it: 'looked at from outside', Simmel's academic life was 'a disaster' (Jung, 1990: 13).

That did not stop Simmel from publishing a massive number of works. These include a completely revised edition of *Die Probleme der Geschichtsphilosophie* (1905), *Die Philosophie des Geldes* (*The Philosophy of Money*) (1900), *Kant* (1904), *Schopenhauer und Nietzsche* (1907) and a number of shorter books. Simmel's *Kant* is still a clear guide to Kant's thinking and the sections in *Schopenhauer und Nietzsche* on Nietzsche are also quite helpful. For sociologists, Simmel's *Soziologie* (1908) is the most important, because he sets out his conception of 'formal sociology'. This lengthy work contains a crucial chapter in which Simmel asks in Kantian fashion, 'How is society possible?' Whereas Kant had answered the question, 'How is nature possible?' by demonstrating that the a priori category of causality makes it so, Simmel answered that a similar type of formal category – 'interaction' – makes society possible (Simmel, 1992: 43–47, 59; see also Adair-Toteff, 1994: 3–8). Simmel's sociology, like Kant's philosophy, is formal; and like Kant, Simmel emphasizes methodology. Although this approach was not universally acknowledged, it was to have great impact. Leopold von Wiese claimed that between 1908, when Simmel's *Soziologie* appeared, and 1926, three-quarters of the sociology published focused on methodology (von Wiese, 1926: 10).

Although Simmel is frequently and correctly regarded as one of the major founders of classical German sociology, some sociologists thought he was too philosophical. They point particularly to what they saw as his abandonment of empirical work for his later metaphysical writings (see, for example, von Wiese, 1926: 84–85). Even though he wrote on standard philosophical topics such as ethics and the philosophy of history, he was never exactly like other Neo-Kantian professors. Some of them looked down on his 'Kulturphilosophie' and some of them thought even less of his later 'Lebensphilosophie' ('Philosophy of Life'). If other professors did not sufficiently appreciate Simmel, many students did. They found him a wonderful lecturer. His topics were eclectic and unconventional – he presented lectures and papers on flirting, on shame; he wrote books on Goethe and Michelangelo; and his style was more popular than pedantic. In his obituary, Georg Lukacs praised Simmel's brilliance but added that because he was a great stimulator, he had no students like Hermann Cohen, Heinrich Rickert, or Edmund Husserl. But he also insisted that without Simmel's sociology, the sociologies of Weber, Troeltsch and Sombart would have been impossible (Lukacs, 1918: 144, 149).

Simmel failed to obtain a full professorship, despite efforts to help him by leading figures such as Weber. The reasons were varied – his non-standard scholarly interests, his unusual and engaging style, his often female or foreign audience, his Jewishness. Only with the advent of the First World War did Simmel receive an appointment to Strasbourg, only to find that the war curtailed most of the university work. He died of cancer on 26 September 1918.

Werner Sombart

As Werner Jung pointed out, little was known about Simmel's 'external biography' (Jung, 1990: 11). Even less is known about Werner Sombart. He was born in Ermsleben near the Harz Mountains on 19 January 1863. Like Tönnies, Sombart's early personal sympathy with socialists and his interest in the socialist movement hindered his academic career. His book on socialism, which first appeared in 1896, and his *Proletariat* were considered socialist in orientation, but his *Der moderne Kapitalismus*, which was first published in 1902, was not. In this work, Sombart attempted to uncover the origins of capitalism. He saw it in the modernization and rationalization of work; he located it primarily in the larger cities; and he found it in the increased striving for profit. Sombart's interest in the genesis of capitalism and the emphasis on rationality link this book with Weber's more famous work on the origins of capitalism – *Die Protestantische Ethik*. But there are more dissimilarities than similarities: Whereas Sombart's work is massive, totalling more than 1,300 pages, Weber's has fewer than 200 pages. Sombart surveyed a plethora of areas and interests, whereas Weber was far more focused. Sombart saw modern rationality as only one part of a complex; while Weber saw it as the defining factor. But Weber seemed largely convinced by his findings and was also able to be convincing.

Der moderne Kapitalismus was just the first of many of Sombart's attempts to explain capitalism, so that by 1928, this work had grown to more than 3,000 pages and had been augmented by a number of other books. In 1911 Sombart published *Die Juden und das Wirtschaftsleben* (*The Jews and Economic Life*), and took issue with Weber's belief in the origins of capitalism in early Protestantism, claiming instead that the origins were found in the Jews (Sombart, 1911). In *Luxus und Kapitalismus* (*Luxury and Capitalism*), Sombart saw the origins of capitalism in the early desires for luxuries, and insisted that women were responsible for these desires (Sombart, 1913c). Yet in *Krieg und Kapitalismus* (*War and Capitalism*) he blamed the rise of capitalism on the need to outfit an army, develop weapons and build ships (Sombart, 1913a). Finally, he maintained that the bourgeois prompted the rise of capitalism. In a letter to Sombart, Weber insisted that like *Die Juden*, virtually every word of *Der Bourgeois* (Sombart, 1913b) was wrong. Yet, he acknowledged having experienced pleasure and enjoyment in reading both books (Weber, 2003: 414–15). Many people seemed to agree with Weber: on the one hand, Sombart offered too many accounts of the same phenomena; yet on the other hand he seemed to offer interesting if not compelling stories. This scattered approach prompted Lawrence Scaff to write 'If one popular explanation of capitalism grew stale and trite, Sombart was always willing to try another' (Scaff, 1989: 203).

After a short period as an 'outsider', Sombart became respected and so regarded as an 'insider'. He was a professor at Berlin from 1906 until 1931. He was a contributor to Weber's *Grundriß* and also contributed six(!) entries in Alfred Vierkandt's *Handwörterbuch der Soziologie* (*Dictionary of Sociology*).[5] As Sombart stated in his paper in the D.G.S., he objected to modern technology,

---

5 These were: *Arbeiter* ('Worker') (1–14); *Beruf* ('Calling') (25–31); *Grundformen des menschlichen Zusammenlebens* ('Basic Forms of Human Communal Life') (221–39); *Kapitalismus* ('Capitalism') (258–77); *Städtische Siedlungen* ('Urban Settlement') (527–33); and *Wirtschaft* ('Economy') (652–59). Not even Vierkandt or Tönnies had as many (four each) (Vierkandt, 1931).

just as he objected to commercialism. In his patriotic contribution to the war effort, Sombart contrasted the Germans, who exulted in the heroic and the sacrificial, to the British, who embraced the commercial and the comfortable (Sombart, 1915). By the 1930s, his views had taken on Nazi ideological colourings and there remained few scholars who held him in any regard. Sombart died on 18 May 1941.

Max Weber

Max Weber was born in Erfurt on 21 April 1864 and spent most of his boyhood years in Berlin. As the son of a relatively successful politician, Weber was able to see and to meet a number of notable politicians and professors, including Wilhelm Dilthey, Theodor Mommsen and Heinrich von Treitschke. As well as studying economics and law at Heidelberg, he attended Kuno Fischer's philosophy classes. In 1889, he received his doctorate, for which he had submitted a dissertation on trade in medieval Italian cities; and in 1891 he submitted a work on Roman agrarian history for his 'Habilitation'. The following year, he was appointed extraordinary professor at Berlin and the next year moved to Freiburg, where he occupied the Chair of Political Economy. In the same year he married Marianne, who was to become a highly regarded scholar and a champion of women's rights. More importantly for our purposes, she edited a number of Weber's posthumously published writings and provided us with an interesting, if rather biased, account of Weber's life and work (Weber, 1926). Weber was called to Heidelberg in 1896, but the following year he began to suffer from mental illness. By 1903 he had recovered enough to return to writing, but decided that he could no longer teach. The same year he resigned his post at Heidelberg.

In 1904, Max and Marianne Weber travelled to the USA, so that Max could present a paper at the World Exhibition in St Louis. They had planned to make the trip an extended one and Max was particularly intrigued by the great cities, such as New York and Chicago. Also in 1904, Max, along with Werner Sombart and Edgar Jaffé, took over the editorship of the *Archiv für Sozialwissenschaft und Sozialpolitik*. Weber wrote most of his essays on methodology between 1904 and 1906, but 1904 and 1905 were the years when he published his *Protestantische Ethik und der Geist des Kapitalismus* in two instalments in the *Archiv*. This was a major work and immediately drew notice, not all of it favourable. Weber's claim was that the origins of capitalism could, to a large degree, be found in Luther's notion of *Beruf* or 'calling'. Instead of the monk alone being 'called', Luther argued that all people were called to work. Calvin built upon this and maintained that one should work solely for the greater glory of God. But in his doctrine of predestination, Calvin contended that no one could know for certain whether he or she had been chosen to be a member of the elect or to be eternally damned. However, Calvin suggested that the riches that people accrued in working for God's glory could be taken as a possible sign of their election. Weber argued further that the rationality of the Calvinist was emphasized by Ben Franklin. But here, his emphasis was not on the *piety* of saving but on the *morality* of frugality. Modern capitalism had lost the piety and the morality of working, so that people were now working solely in order to accumulate more and more money. What had once been merely a means to an end had become an end in itself.

Weber expanded his work on economic ethics in religion. These studies were first published in the *Archiv*, then in the three volumes of *Religionssoziologie*, in which the Protestant study formed the first major chapter. Weber was also hard at work on the *Grundriß*. He did not want the title of Editor, but in effect that is what he was. He had first proposed that the work be called the *Handbuch der politische Ökonomie* (*Handbook of Political Economy*), but because of legal problems he had to change the name. His original plan was to ask a number of leading experts to contribute, so that he would write just a few contributions, but because of time constraints and problems with the unevenness of some of the contributions, his portion continued to expand. His contribution was published after his death and is now known mostly as *Wirtschaft und Gesellschaft* (*Economy and Society*). This incredibly important book includes not only his 'basic concepts' of sociology but also his sociology of law, his sociology of domination and his political sociology.

During the First World War, Weber worked and wrote tirelessly to help ensure that Germany would win. He objected strenuously to the increase in submarine warfare, arguing (correctly) that as a consequence, the USA would enter the war. While he was concerned that the USA's involvement would help defeat Germany, Weber's even greater concern was with the Soviet Union. He feared the Soviet bureaucratic and socialist power behind the Soviet forces. Weber addressed the issue of socialism in a speech he gave in Vienna in the summer of 1918. He was there to try teaching for one semester. While he evidently enjoyed teaching again, he found it difficult to be away from his wife and his country. He returned to Germany and took up a Chair in Munich. There he gave two important speeches – *Wissenschaft als Beruf* (*Science as Vocation*) in 1917; and *Politik als Beruf* (*Politics as Vocation*) in 1919. In these lectures, Weber set out his conditions for the scholars and the politicians who choose their calling and he emphasized the notions of clarity and responsibility.

Some scholars have argued that Weber was an 'outsider', that he was a failed would-be politician and that his notion of leadership led to certain tenets of Nazi ideology. This is not the place to take issue with these claims. What is irrefutable is that Weber had a powerful personality and a keen and wide-ranging intellect. While he founded no 'school', his influence has been immense. Weber died in Munich on 14 June 1920 at the age of 56.

Ernst Troeltsch

Ernst Troeltsch was born in Augsburg on 17 February 1865. From his physician father Troeltsch learned about natural science and about the importance of clarity and precision, traits that were too often missing from his contemporaries (see Troeltsch, 1925a: 3). He received his doctorate in theology in 1891 at Göttingen and his 'Habilitation' there in the same year. In his Habilitationsschrift, Troeltsch looked to the early Reformation to see how the opposing notions of reason and revelation played out. In 1892, Troeltsch became a professor at Bonn and in 1894 he was called to Heidelberg, where he became Professor of Systematic Theology. This title should not give rise to the assumption that Troeltsch was a fanatical believer in and defender of Christianity. In his 1902 *Die Absolutheit des Christentums und die Religionsgeschichte* (*The Absoluteness of Christianity and the History of Religions*), Troeltsch made efforts to show that while Christianity lacked the absolute that so many theologians had claimed for it, it nonetheless marked the contemporary high point of religious thinking. This work also served to underscore Troeltsch's main theological interest – the history of theology. Two lengthy works from 1906 demonstrate that this interest is not only theological but also sociological. In *Protestantisches Christentum und Kirche in der Neuzeit* (*Protestant Christianity in Modern Times*) and in *Die Bedeutung des Protestantismus für die Entstehung der modernen Welt* (*The Significance of Protestantisum for the Development of the Modern World*), Troeltsch showed how the Protestant emphasis on the individual helped pave the way for the Enlightenment and thus for modernity. Troeltsch's concern with the Enlightenment emphasis on reason is also apparent in his work on Leibniz and Kant. This is evident in 'Das Historische in Kant's Religionsphilosophie' ('The Historical in Kant's Philosophy of Religion'), which was published in *Kant-Studien* in 1904. He also contributed the article on the philosophy of religion in the *Festschrift* for the famous Heidelberg historian of philosophy, Kuno Fischer. By 1908, Troeltsch's theological interests had become even more historical, as well as sociological, and in that year he began to publish sections of his massive *Die Soziallehren der christlichen Kirchen in der Archiv für Sozialwissenschaft und Sozialpolitik*. Troeltsch continued publishing instalments until 1910, after which he completed the work and published it in its entirety in 1912. The English translation, *The*

Social Teaching of the Christian Churches, minimizes Troeltsch's emphasis on the various 'teachings'. He demonstrated that no single doctrine or dogma runs through Christianity; instead, different ones dominated at different times, and that these represent the needs and desires of different groups of believers. To this end, he analysed the differences between Early Church and the institutional (Catholic) Church and between the 'old' Protestant Church and the New Protestant Church. Moreover, Troeltsch built upon Weber's distinction between church and sect to investigate the radical individuality and extreme otherworldly beliefs of the mystic.

In 1904, Troeltsch and his wife accompanied Max and Marianne Weber to the USA, where he presented a paper at the World Congress. Illness in the family caused Troeltsch and his wife to return to Germany soon after the Congress. Their developing friendship with the Webers made it possible for the Troeltschs to move into the upper storey of the Weber house in Heidelberg in 1910. The previous year, Troeltsch had been offered two different professorships in Berlin, which he turned down. Weber applauded this decision because Troeltsch was so important to Heidelberg University. However, during the First World War, differences of opinion regarding the treatment of prisoners brought about a cooling of the friendship between Troeltsch and Weber. When, in 1914, Troeltsch was again offered a position in Berlin, he accepted it immediately, but did not move until the following year. Beginning in 1910, Troeltsch had lectured in philosophy, and the Chair he took in Berlin was very prestigious, previous incumbents having been Wilhelm Dilthey and Georg Hegel. Like Friedrich Schleiermacher, Troeltsch was a theologian and a philosopher, and he intended that his *Glaubenslehre* (*Doctrine of Faith*) (Troeltsch, 1925c) be patterned after Schleiermacher's two-volume work of the same name. But Troeltsch's work was less doctrinal and more philosophical than Schleiermacher's.

The war accentuated Troeltsch's interests in politics and political thinking and he became a member of the Weimar government. He was also very active as a political journalist: two collections of his writings were published posthumously: *Spektator-Briefe* (*Spectator's Letters*) (Troeltsch, 1924b); and *Deutscher Geist und Westeuropa* (*German Spirit and West Europe*) (Troeltsch, 1925b). In these writings, Troeltsch commented not only on the political activities during the war and its revolutionary aftermath but also on their cultural significance. The war also prompted Troeltsch to investigate the notion of relativism in history. He published some of his conclusions in *Der Historismus und seine Probleme* (*Historicism and its Problems*) (Troeltsch, 1922) but the second volume was never completed because of his death. Consequently, we have historical and critical sketches of the various problems, but no concrete answers. The closest to answers that Troeltsch provided are in the collection of essays that were published posthumously as *Der Historismus und seine Überwindung* (*Historicism and its Overcoming*) (Troeltsch, 1924a).

Like Tönnies, Simmel, Sombart and Weber, Troeltsch was ultimately a sociologist who was keenly interested in almost all of society's cultural manifestations. But Troeltsch may have been the most historically oriented of the five. He was the youngest; Simmel and Weber predeceased him, whereas Tönnies and Sombart outlived him by many years. Troeltsch died on 1 February 1923.

While the five had their individual strengths and interests, all were convinced of the necessity of establishing sociology as a science. And, by 1909–1910, all had agreed that presenting papers at the inaugural conference of the D.G.S. was a major step in achieving this. So what was the D.G.S. and how did it come about?

The Deutsche Gesellschaft für Soziologie

By 1908 the study of social interactions, or sociology, had begun to receive more attention and more of its practitioners wanted greater respectability accorded to it. A sociological society already existed in France and in 1907 Rudolf Goldshied founded the Soziologische Gesellschaft in Vienna. It was time for one to be formed in Germany and Tönnies, Simmel, Sombart and Weber wanted to do it. Among these four there were personal as well as professional relations. Although Weber had a few disagreements with Tönnies, he thought highly of Tönnies and his work. Early in June 1908, Weber wrote to Tönnies asking him to write a review of Simmel's *Soziologie* for the *Archiv* (Weber, 1990: 583). He also compared Tönnies' lack of advancement to Simmel's, commiserating that one should not have to be 50 years old and still not have received a call to a regular professorship (Weber, 1990: 584). Towards the end of July, Weber wrote to Tönnies again to ask that he review Simmel's book. Weber acknowledged Tönnies' reluctance to review books, but insisted that his opinion of it would be of great value (Weber, 1990: 607). Tönnies stayed with the Webers during the Third International Congress for Philosophy that was held in Heidelberg between 1 and 5 September of the same year. Weber heard two of Tönnies' lectures there. He wrote to Jaffé that Tönnies' paper on Comte was 'indeed stimulating' but found nothing 'unconditionally new' in it; but he insisted that Tönnies' lecture, 'A New Method of Moral Statistics', was exceptional and that it was the result of 20 great years of research. Excluding *Gemeinschaft und Gesellschaft*, it was the best that Tönnies had done and it would be a *Zierde* (an 'ornament' or honour) for the *Archiv* were it to appear there.[6] Weber also seemed pleased that Tönnies finally got an extraordinary professorship in Kiel in December 1908 (Weber, 1990: 710).

Weber's relations with Sombart were also close. He valued Sombart and frequently relied on his expert opinion (Weber, 1990: 7; 114, 207). Furthermore, Weber was incensed by the personal and destructive review by Hans Delbrück of Sombart's *Der moderne Kapitalismus* (Weber, 1990: 232–35, 603). Their major disagreements came because of Sombart's penchant for writing books and articles from a personal point of view, in which he pressed for 'ethical' or 'ideal' standpoints which, in Weber's view, had no place in the *Archiv* (Weber, 1990: 606). By 1908, Weber and Sombart both had resigned as official Co-Editors of the *Archiv*, although they continued to assist Jaffé.

Simmel was also on close professional and personal terms with Weber. Simmel's wife, Gertrud, and Marianne Weber were quite close, partly as a result of their shared assessment of the role of women in modern society. Although Simmel disagreed with Marianne on this, he dedicated his *Goethe* (1913) to her. Weber's attempts to help Simmel to get a professorship in Heidelberg are fairly well documented. He encouraged Simmel when appropriate, intervened when he could and stood by his friend when Berlin denied the appointment on stupid religious and bigoted grounds.[7]

At the end of 1908, Tönnies, Simmel, Sombart and Weber were engaged in forming the Deutsche Gesellschaft für Soziologie, although Weber did not attend the first meeting on its organization that was held in Berlin on 3 January 1909. However, he began to be intimately connected with its organization by early February. In a letter to Jaffé, Weber wondered how they should publicize the D.G.S. in the *Archiv* and whether the journal could serve as its official organ (Weber, 1994: 44–45). However, he had considerable reservations about serving in some official capacity. The executive committee did not originally include Weber but did include Simmel and Tönnies, along with Alfred Vierkandt, Heinrich Herkner and Herman Beck (Weber, 1994: 58, Note 3). Another meeting followed on 7 March in Berlin, when Weber was elected Treasurer. Weber was pressing for a decision in the autumn of that year on the final make-up of the Executive Committee and was uncertain whether Herkner would refuse the Chairmanship or not.[8]

---

6 Weber, 1990: 654. Nothing came of this and it appeared in a shortened form in the Conference Report and in full in *Schmöllers Jahrbuch* in 1909.

7 Weber, 1990: 298, 457, 469; see also the editorial remarks to Weber's letter to Georg Jellineck of 21 March 1908; Weber, 1990: 467–469.

8 Weber, 1994: 71–72. He did refuse it and Beck held it from 1909 until 1914. Tönnies, Simmel and Sombart most frequently held the Chairmanship.

During the early stages of its foundation, the D.G.S. was in flux, but many of its members were trying their best to strengthen it. For example, Weber tried several times to get well known and respected scholars such as political economists Lujo Brentano and Carl Johannes Fuchs to join, but apparently without success (Weber, 1994: 93–96, 107–108, 138, 145). Attempts to arrange for Alfred Weber and Franz Eulenburg to give papers at the first conference also failed. Further meetings of the D.G.S. followed in Leipzig in the autumn and spring. The list of speakers was beginning to be firmed up. Simmel, Tönnies, Sombart and Troeltsch had made commitments, as had Eberhard Gotthein and Alfred Ploetz. The question remained as to where to hold the conference. As a Berliner, Simmel naturally pressed for Berlin, but others pushed for Frankfurt. Weber agreed that the permanent seat of the D.G.S. should be in Berlin, but he seemed open to suggestions for a venue for the conference elsewhere. Weber insisted on two key provisions in his proposed statutes for the D.G.S. The first was that only people who worked in the area of sociology or closely related fields could be full members of the D.G.S. And the second was that since the goal of the D.G.S. was to achieve scientific results, the D.G.S. should repudiate any and all 'practical' goals as a matter of fundamental principle – by this, Weber meant that the D.G.S. should not pursue any political, ethical, or religious goals.[9] He had nothing against such goals, provided that they were undertaken in the appropriate spheres, and a scientific society would not and should not be such a sphere.

By early July, the decision had been made that the conference should be held at Frankfurt, and an announcement was published in the *Archiv* (Band 31, Heft 2, 1910: 710). Simmel, Tönnies, Sombart, Troeltsch and Weber were scheduled to speak, as were Gotthein, Ploetz and Voigt. It was Weber's suggestion that they add Kantorowicz to speak with Voigt on law (see Weber, 1994: 607, 610, 613–14). It was also Weber's suggestion that there could be sub-groups on statistics, legal philosophy–sociology and economic theory (Weber, 1994: 636). Kantorowicz spoke, but the discussion of sub-groups was postponed.

9 See Weber, 1994: 548–53 (esp. 548). Number 1 reads: 'Under the name German Society for Sociology an association is founded that has its seat in Berlin. Its purpose is the continuation of sociological knowledge through the arrangement of pure scientific investigations and enquiries, through publication and support of pure scientific works and through the organization of periodically occurring sociological conferences. It provides equal room for all scientific directions and methods of sociology and rejects the representation of any practical (ethical, religious, political, aesthetic, etc.) goals' (*VDG*, 1911: V). Weber provided an addendum to the Statutes in late September 1910 (Weber, 1994: 626–628).

The Major Papers of the First D.G.S. Conference

The first conference of the Deutsche Gesellschaft für Soziologie took place beginning on Wednesday 19 October 1910 and continuing until Saturday 22 October. Simmel began the *Begrüßungsabend* (Evening of Greeting) with his paper, 'Soziologie der Geselligkeit'.

Simmel

The term *Geselligkeit* can be translated as 'sociability', 'sociality', 'company', or 'social life'. When Simmel writes of the *Wesen* (essence) of society, one is inclined to think that Simmel believed that 'society' is some kind of 'entity', but this inclination is wrong. While he regarded a society as 'a higher unity', he did not regard it as an object, a thing. Thus, in the opposition between the conception of society as something that is inborn and something that is 'formed', he favoured the latter. By 'formed' he meant something like how a landscape is 'formed' from individual objects such a house, a brook, trees, etc.; but he did not mean that society is 'formed' from individual people as objects. Simmel was too much of a Kantian for that, so his interest was in the *relations* between people. Whereas Kant's concern was with causality between objects, Simmel's preoccupation was with interaction between individuals. He emphasized this in the notion of *Wechselwirkung*, or 'interaction' (*VDG*, 1911: 8, 9, 10, 11). This term, like Kant's 'causality', is a 'category', but Simmel's category is a sociological one. *Wechselwirkung* is sometimes rendered as 'reciprocal action' and there is much to be said for this, since 'interaction' does not convey the same sense of continuous involvement. However, 'reciprocal' has a sense of equality that is often lacking in Simmel. For Simmel, even more than for Weber, social activity is rarely peaceful, but is often dominated by conflict. Indeed, for many years Simmel's reputation rested on his discussions of conflict.[10] In this paper, however, Simmel was less concerned about conflict than about social interaction. This social interaction is often predicated on opposites. He concentrated on the moods of individuals and specified the motions of getting into and falling out of a good mood, of becoming excited, of becoming depressed. These are the lightness and darkness of social interactions, and Simmel stressed that different social settings allow or encourage different social interactions. He noted that a woman will flirt in a specific social setting – one in which she feels fairly safe and comfortable – but not in some other social

10 Featherstone, 1991: 1, Jung: 1990: 83. Simmel's 'Sociology of Conflict' appeared in *The American Journal of Sociology* in 1903/1904 and 'Conflict' appeared in books in 1955 and 1968 (Frisby, 1991: 240–41).

setting. Simmel's example also serves to underscore two further points. First, Simmel's social interactions are often fleeting and sometimes playful; they are never permanent and they are sometimes tragic. Second, a person will interact with other people depending on the role played by and the function of that person and the other people. A person has different roles – a business person; a political actor; a family member. In other places, Simmel emphasizes that a Catholic will interact differently with other Catholics from the way he or she interacts with Protestants. So, social reality is constantly subject to change. We can know people only under the conditions of social interaction.

Simmel saw no social 'reality' in the sense that society 'exists'. As he put it, all sociability is only a *symbol* of life (*VDG*, 1911: 14). Its reality is found in the continual ebb and flow of human interaction. He allowed that in a sense we are 'products' of this continuous social interaction; but he also maintained that we are capable of determining large portions of our own lives, that we are able to influence the people around us. In Simmel's view, this underscores the notion of *Wechselwirkung*: 'societal interaction' influences us and, conversely, we influence 'social interaction'.

Tönnies

The title of Tönnies' paper says almost all: 'Wege und Ziele der Soziologie' ('Ways and Goals of Sociology'). This is almost entirely because his main interests were the methods and the goals of sociology; and to investigate them, he looked backwards and forwards. He looked back to the beginnings of sociology, specifically to August Comte and Herbert Spencer, both of whom were instrumental in founding sociology – Comte with the name and Spencer with some fundamental principles. However, Tönnies took issue with Comte, partly because his sociology is far more metaphysical than Comte himself acknowledged (*VDG*, 1911: 23). Comte argued that human history could be divided into three phases or stages of development. Tönnies took this to mean that the first was theological, that is, virtually every issue was decided on theological grounds; and the second was 'metaphysical', that is, issues were considered in the light of philosophical reasoning. It is only with the advent of the third, the positivist period that matters were considered on their own merits without otherworldly trappings. Tönnies believed that this triad was itself somewhat metaphysical, and he meant by that Hegelian, with Hegel's supposed thesis-antithesis-synthesis dialectical process.[11] Furthermore, Tönnies suggested

11 Some Hegelian scholars object to this characterization, insisting that it is an oversimplification of Hegel's dialectic, or pointing out that it was not Hegel who used this formulation but one of his later, lesser-known followers.

that this was also too artificial and that by insisting on it, Comte was not following his own scientific principles.

Tönnies objected to Spencer because of his 'monism'. By this he meant that in his view Spencer sought to apply evolutionary theory to everything. However, Tönnies also thought highly of Spencer's work, noting that his writings were powerful and carefully thought out. In this, Spencer and Comte differed from many historical thinkers who were too concerned with ideas and ideals.

Tönnies was concerned that too often, ideas were the driving force behind social theories. He argued that this was wrong and that instead, we should look to reality. By this he did not mean that we should repudiate thought; indeed, he insisted that one of the great tasks of the sociologist was to construct concepts to explain social reality. In doing so, Tönnies was not only in accord with Kant's thinking but also with that of Heinrich Rickert. The difference lay in that Tönnies wanted to provide accounts of social situations and social interactions; Rickert, by contrast, sought to provide concepts to explain historical events and historical connections.

Regarding ideals, Tönnies was troubled by the human inclination to want to see things as they *should be*, rather than examining them as they *are* (*VDG*, 1911: 23), which meant looking forward. Like Weber and Sombart, Tönnies insisted that the social scientist must focus on social reality, not on social 'ideality' and, like them he rejected Comte's idea that sociology could forecast the future accurately. That is why Tönnies rejected what he called *Zukunfts-gedanken* or 'ideas of the future'. This is not to say that he totally dismissed the idea that sociological investigations could not be of some help for considerations of the future. Like Weber and Sombart, Tönnies placed a large value on the use of statistics in making it possible to project from the past and the present to what might occur in the future. This did not imply inevitability, either of the Hegelian idealistic type or the Marxist materialistic type; it was closer to David Hume's contention that from similar causes we can consider the likelihood that similar effects will follow.

Tönnies did not reject concerns about the future as being irrelevant, but merely inappropriate for scientific considerations. That is why he insisted that as *sociologists*, his audience needed to concern themselves with what *is*. As *non-sociologists* – i.e. when not investigating social interactions – they could and possibly ought to be concerned with what *should be*. Tönnies' biography is full of instances in which he fought for social justice and social equality and for the elimination of prejudice and discrimination. But those he saw as the concerns of the political person, not of the sociologist, who needs to be concerned with man. In his paper for the conference, Tönnies quoted with approval Goethe's appropriation of Alexander Pope's dictum that the proper study of mankind is man (*VDG*, 1911: 37). He also acknowledged that this imperative form is similar to Socrates' constant use of the Oracle's command to 'know oneself'. Yet whereas the historical Socrates was concerned in large part with knowing himself, Tönnies was like the Platonic Socrates, who is interested in man's place in social settings. Plato's concern in *The Republic* is the ideal state; Tönnies' concern was with real society, and that meant investigating social realities in all their *historical* and *present* forms.

That Tönnies was successful in setting out his conception of the proper sociological methods and goals is supported by the comment made by Gerhart von Schulze-Gävernitz, who said that Tönnies' lecture was the best treatment of sociology and its essence to date. Schulze-Gävernitz said this at the beginning of his comments on Sombart's paper and it was in keeping with his character that Tönnies, as Chairman, reminded Schulze-Gävernitz that they were supposed to be discussing Sombart's paper, not his.

Weber

If the title of Tönnies' paper is sufficient indication of its contents, the title of Weber's *Geschäftsbericht* ('Business Report') is positively misleading. Except at the beginning and at the end, his paper has virtually nothing to do with the number of members or the finances of the D.G.S. Instead, it is a collection of interesting ideas which can be grouped into two areas. First, Weber urges the Society to investigate the nature and the effects of newspapers. Second, he suggests that the Society analyse the functions of associations. In both cases, Weber utilizes a principle that he often employs, namely comparisons between German newspapers and those of other countries and the various associations in Germany compared to those in other western countries.

Weber intended to introduce several major areas of discussion: the changes in the Society's constitution; and concrete research projects. All are, of course, connected to the term 'sociology', which, he said, is an unpopular name (*VDG*, 1911: 39). This is true, but it is also a reflection of Weber's antipathy towards it. Karl Jaspers can generally be assumed to have been a reliable witness to Weber's thoughts, having had a long-term, close friendship with him, so we can assume that Jaspers was right when he reported that Weber said in public 'Most of what goes by the name of sociology is swindle' (Jaspers, 1932: 53). Weber may have had in mind that there was still a huge tendency for 'sociologists' to make value judgements, something he had long fought against. With this remark, he echoed Tönnies' call to reject the propaganda of 'practical ideas'. These must be fundamentally and definitively rejected.

Like Tönnies, Weber insisted that the D.G.S. must be 'party-less'. This meant that the D.G.S. must reject any question of the value of the ideas, but must focus exclusively on the analysis of the relevant facts. Since he was to speak on the 'essence of the newspaper' (*Zeitungswesen*), Weber added that whether a newspaper deserves such and such a reputation is not relevant; the issue is: how does it come to have this reputation? From what historical and social grounds did this reputation arise?

Weber insisted on a second point: that the D.G.S. was no 'academy' association. With this, he rejected all the prestige of belonging to an elite academy. In his view, the D.G.S. was a working association – anyone interested in working on social problems in this sense was welcome.

Weber's third point was his rejection of what he called *Ressort-Patriotismus*. For sports aficionados, this has the connotation of the Monday morning commentator – the person who, from the safe vantage point of Monday morning is emphatic about what the team should have done or should not have done. Weber had in mind the members of departments, who, from the safety and security of their offices were emphatic about what Germany should and should not do.

From these three points, Weber drew the conclusion that the D.G.S. needed to become decentralized. To this end, he intended to promote sections of the organization, whose members would work independently on specific problems. There was already a movement to start a sub-group devoted to statistics. Weber then moved to his central theme – the study of the essence of the newspaper.

Weber repudiated any discussion of the universal significance of the newspaper industry. Instead, he analysed it comparatively. He did so by comparing it with the ancient publicists and with contemporary newspapers. As in most of his writings, Weber was concerned with the issue of power and he drew upon it in explaining the differences in newspapers from various countries. He used as an illustration the case of an English lord who marries an American woman: newspapers in both countries would be really interested in *Physis und Psyche* ('body and mind'!), but newspapers in Germany would not. He later noted, however, that many newspapers fail to report 'real news' but provide entertainment with sports pages, crossword puzzles and novelettes (*VDG*, 1911: 49). These are themes that represent supra-individual values.

This led Weber to discuss the notion of *Vereine* (associations). Weber briefly discussed the whole range of 'associations', from the *Kegelklub* to political parties and religious sects. The notion of *Kegelklub* carries with it much more than the name, 'bowling club', suggests. It encompasses clubs whose members live in close contact, who share the same values and often the same prejudices. The *Kegelklub* often travels as a group, has regular functions, which are primarily social, and has little to do with sports. To illustrate how 'associations' function, Weber recounted how, when in the USA, he had been told by a doctor, a German nose specialist, that his first patient had said, immediately after introducing himself, that he belonged to the First Baptist Church on a particular street. The patient was making the point was that he was a respectable gentleman and that the doctor need not worry about payment.[12] Belonging to an association confers legitimacy and respectability, regardless of whether it is an English sports club or a German duelling fraternity. It does so whether it is a German singing group or even a *Kegelklub* (*VDG*, 1911: 57). It is, as Weber suggested, a form of 'selection' (*Auslese*).

In conclusion, Weber brought up the topic of research into the essence of the newspaper. He calculated that it would cost some 25,000 Marks, of which 20,000 was contributed by various groups. The D.G.S. would need to raise the remaining 5,000 Marks. This would be for the continuation of specific scientific research work.[13]

Sombart

Sombart divided his paper, 'Technik und Kultur' ('Technology and Culture'), into three parts: one on technology; one on culture; and a longer one on the 'and' (*VDG*, 1911: 63) – but he made it clear that by 'and' he meant the causal interaction between the first two. His paper is intriguing for a variety of reasons. First, he was one of the earliest sociologists to investigate these causal connections. While Simmel and Weber looked at the effects that modern economics had on social life, Sombart focused in his paper specifically on certain effects that technology had on modern culture. Sombart used culture in two senses. First, he considered culture in the narrow sense, applying it to music, arts and cultivation so that when he spoke of modern music, modern art and modern printing he was using 'culture' in this narrow sense. Second, he applied the concept of culture to life in general, to daily life. This is the sense in which he used the term when he discussed modern transport, street lighting, printing, and so forth. It could be this changing back and forth between senses that provoked so much misunderstanding of his topic. The misunderstanding prompted him to add a footnote to the printed copy of his paper, requesting

12 Weber recounted the same example with a number of others to illustrate the same point in *Die protestantische Sekten und der Geist der Kapitalismus*; see *Gesammelte Aufsätze zur Religionssoziologie* (Weber, 1920, I: 209).

13 This did not occur for several reasons. First, Weber continued to have intellectual and political fights with his D.G.S. colleagues; and second, because of his wife Weber got into a protracted public and legal battle over the questions of honour, slander and the use of anonymity in the Press. For a brief account of it, see Käsler, 1988: 17; and the *Einleitung* to Weber's correspondence (Weber, 1994: 5).

that people read his article in the *Archiv für Sozialwissenschaft und Sozialpolitik*, in which he pursued many of the same themes. The misunderstanding also undoubtedly arose because of Sombart's attitude. He ridiculed the pretensions of professors and educated people as a whole and this offended some in his audience. He took pains to include himself as an object of ridicule, but that may not have pacified his critics. But for his critics to dismiss his paper out of disdain would have been a great disservice to him. To forestall this eventuality, Sombart offered a trenchant investigation into the causal connections between technology and culture. He emphasized that his discussion was necessarily limited and provisional and insisted that he could not thoroughly spell out the interrelatedness between the two topics. Furthermore, while he offered what he called the deductive or a priori method, he concentrated on offering examples to help illuminate the discussion. Whether modern inventions – the printing press and the telephone, for example – could have prevented catastrophes such as the destruction of the house of Atreus, or the Crusades – is subject to doubt, but it is clear that Sombart was correct in raising the issue of the relationship between technology and cultural occurrences.

The paper is also intriguing because Sombart was justified in pointing out that many of the technological achievements of which we are proudest are important only if we regard the situations they appear to remedy as a problem. Street lights are necessary only when people roam the streets at night (*VDG*, 1911: 82). Even if Sombart's value judgements about modern city life are dubious and his remarks about women in public are inflammatory, he raised serious issues: Is modern music a reflection of the 'din' (*Lärm*) of city life? Could women have been emancipated from household drudgery without modern technological inventions?[14] Even though his views on modernity seem quaint, if not antiquated, he clearly emphasized that value judgements differ fundamentally from scientific considerations. In this he was in total agreement with his four colleagues, especially Weber. Marianne Weber reported in her biography of Weber that he and Sombart participated in a conference in 1909 where people consistently confused value judgements and scientific enquiries. The discussion of one case prompted Sombart to remark that the matter could not be settled until scientific proof could establish whether blondes or brunettes are prettier (Weber, 1926: 423). Like Weber, Sombart believed that questions of scientific fact can and should be investigated coolly; and that when anyone ventures into questions of values, tempers inevitably rise; and, like Weber, he did not denigrate matters relating to values. He believed that

14 Even though Tönnies made it clear that he preferred the old, traditional rural life, he does not seem as dismissive as Sombart. Sombart's remarks about the evils of technology are similar to those made later by Heidegger.

they are of the utmost importance and, above all, are an area of personal importance.

That many in the audience misunderstood Sombart is evident from the comments on his paper. Some took him to task about his interpretation of Marxism, while others criticized him for making generalizations. Sombart was not discussing Marxism per se, but was pointing out that the materialist conception of history is also connected with technology. Those who made the claim about generalizations seemed to miss Sombart's repeated use of examples and his assertion that given the time limitations, he had had to make some remarks that were more sweeping than he would have liked. Finally, one critic asked whether Sombart maintained that the entire history of logic from Aristotle to Kant depended upon technology. It was not a claim that Sombart made and he emphatically rejected it. Sombart was too good a sociologist to make an elementary error of that sort.

Troeltsch

Troeltsch was addressing a theme that was of life-long interest to him in his paper 'Das stoisch-christliche Naturrecht und das moderne Profane Natur-recht': that of the ethical and social implications of the notion of natural law. Despite the long history of the notion of natural law, it is rather difficult to define. This stems partly from its religious background and partly from its non-religious sources. Regardless of whether they agree with the notion of natural law, virtually all scholars agree that in essence, human life is purposeful. Non-Christians understand that to mean that human beings have some ultimate purpose; and Christians understand that their purpose is to fulfil the goals God has set for them. In both cases, there are laws that are set forth in order to ensure or at least aid in fulfilling those God-set goals. For non-Christians, these laws are man-made; for Christians, they are divine in origin. In both cases, human beings are mandated to follow them; and, in both cases natural law is set against 'positive' law. Briefly, 'positive' law is held to have human origins, which are not to be found in some universal notion of reason or purpose-fulness, but in the particular and peculiar rules and regulations of communities. Or, to give a slightly different explanation, the source of 'positive' law is human, while the source of natural law is divine or metaphysical. As a result, positive law is criticized as being relativistic, in that any community's positive laws are binding. Furthermore, critics of positive law contend that there cannot be any ultimate tribunal to which a community's laws can be brought, so if one community legally endorses acts to which other communities object, nothing can be done to force change. All are 'equal'.

24

Troeltsch was not interested in positive law, only in natural law. In his paper, he contended that there are two types of laws: 'natural laws' govern real social interactions, while 'ideal laws' postulate an 'ideal realm' (*VDG*, 1911: 166–68). He maintained that it is impossible to unify the two, or, in some Hegelian fashion, raise them up to a third. Troeltsch's main interest was not so much in 'ideal laws' as in the ways in which the ideal is made manifest in the real world. He made considerable use of the two distinctions he made in *Soziallehren*. He divided Christianity into four 'ages'. The first, 'the old Church' extended from the time of Jesus, through Paul and into the very early Middle Ages. The second is medieval Catholicism. The third is early Protestantism, encompassing Lutheranism and Calvinism. Troeltsch did not deal with the fourth age – 'modern' Protestantism. The other distinction is one he borrowed from Weber – the distinction between 'church' and 'sect'. Weber suggested that a 'church' tends to be an institution to which a person is 'obligated' to belong in order to receive grace. By contrast, Weber stressed that a person voluntarily becomes and remains a member of a 'sect', so that it lacks the institutionalization of a 'church' (Weber, 1920: 211, 221).

To the church and the sect, Troeltsch added the mystic, who rejects the 'objectivization' of the religious in any form, be it cults, rites, myths, or dogma; and anything that diminishes or hinders the immediacy and inward presence of religious feeling (Troeltsch, 1912: 850, 854). The mystic strives for enthusiasm and visions, for the orgiastic and the hallucinatory (Troeltsch, 1912: 850). The mystic wishes to reduce the distance between man and creature, to lose the self in God. The mystic is often a pantheist (Troeltsch, 1912: 855). Troeltsch based much of his reasoning on Erwin Rhode's *Psyche* and William James's *Varieties of Religious Experience*.[15] In the paper, Troeltsch emphasized the sect's property of rigour and almost total refusal to compromise; and the mystic's sole interest in mystical union and the almost complete rejection of history and institutions (*VDG*, 1911: 172–73).

Having made these historical and methodological distinctions, Troeltsch turned his attention to the history of natural law. When the Stoa replaced the positive law of the polis with their version of natural law, they did away with the various differences between states, races and the like (*VDG*, 1911: 175–76). The Stoa realized that this was an ideal, so they differentiated between an absolute and a relative natural law.[16] The Christians took over the ideal and

15 Troeltsch, 1912: 852. William James (1902), *The Varieties of Religious Experience*. Erwin Rohde (1907), *Psyche: Seelencult und Unsterblichkeitsglaube der Griechen*. Tübingen: J.C.B. Mohr (Paul Siebeck).

16 The distinction need not be explored here. An account can be found in Adair-Toteff, 2005.

believed that the natural order of things could be discovered by reason (*VDG*, 1911: 179). It was St Thomas who set out the Catholic doctrine that through the use of reason, individuals could come to understand and to participate in God's plan for Creation.

In addition to the part that natural law plays in Catholicism Troeltsch observed that natural law plays an important role in Protestantism. It is found in its emphasis on individuality, individual calling and individual responsibility (*VDG*, 1911: 184–88). It is also found in the modern world, for example, in the modern doctrine of natural rights. While the modern conception rejects the religious foundation of natural law, it embraces the same moralistic tones. Furthermore, the older religious notion of natural law and the modern doctrine of natural rights share the same belief in the ultimate purposefulness of the world – a world in which reason and good triumph (*VDG*, 1911: 189). Troeltsch concluded by asserting that the modern profane doctrine of natural law has to face the same difficulties and has to undertake the same struggles as the old Stoic–Christian idea (*VDG*, 1911: 191–92).

Tönnies was the first to comment on Troeltsch's paper. While he acknowledged Troeltsch's expertise in church history and in the delineation of the three types, he maintained that Troeltsch did not take into consideration historical materialism and did not pay enough attention to Hobbes. Weber responded by defending his 'friend and colleague', hinting that Troeltsch's paper was not the appropriate place in which to discuss the role of economics, and noted that he dealt with that in his published writings. Weber continued by arguing that the Church and even to some extent the sects of the Middle Ages were found only in the city; that the power of the Pope was tied to cities and that the mendicant orders (*Bettelorden*) could only have existed in urban areas.

Simmel thought there may be a paradox in the claim that there is a social significance. The paradox seems to appear because there are no *social* relations, only the relation to God. As he put it 'We are all children of the same Father'. Building on this, Martin Buber questioned whether mysticism can be a sociological category, since it has very little to do with natural law. He contended that mysticism is really religious solipsism.

A most special moment of the conference came at the conclusion of Troeltsch's session. Simmel, as Chairman, asked Troeltsch if he wished to have the final word, and he declined. Weber must have prompted him, for Troeltsch quickly announced that Weber 'said that the devil should take him if he did not speak' (*Herr Kollege Weber sagt, der Teufel solle mich holen, wenn ich nicht spreche*). This prompted laughter. Again there was laughter when Troeltsch added that 'considering this authority', there was nothing he could do but speak. It was unclear whether Troeltsch was regarding Weber or the devil as 'this authority'.

The Remaining Papers of the First D.G.S. Conference

Four other papers were presented at the conference. Alfred Ploetz gave a paper on the concept of race and society, in which he stressed two opposing strands of thinking: first, the notion of the struggle for survival; and second, the notion of support from human society (*VDG*, 1911: 127–31). Several people objected to the notion of selection and pointed to famous people who contributed enormously to culture and society, despite being handicapped (*VDG*, 1911: 149–50). Tönnies asked whether Moses Mendelssohn was a 'variation' and Goldscheid asked whether society would have been better had Mendelssohn been 'selected out' (*VDG*, 1911: 160). Ploetz replied no, that he had been misunderstood. He had not meant to imply that the weaker should be eliminated (*VDG*, 1911: 150, 161). It was clear to most of the audience that Ploetz either did not understand the connection between race and society, or that he could not explain it satisfactorily.

Eberhard Gothein's paper was far more satisfactory. Gothein, Weber's successor at Heidelberg, presented a paper on the 'Soziologie der Panik' ('Sociology of Panic'). In this clear and intriguing paper Gothein noted that panic tends to be an isolating feeling, in that the panicky person feels cut off from others and helpless. However, Gothein alluded to Simmel's preoccupation in the first part of *Soziologie* to the less than clear-cut boundary between the individual and the masses (*VDG*, 1911: 216–19). Gothein further differentiated between 'natural' panic, which appeared to him to be a result of something naturally occurring; and 'fantasy or suggestion panic', which seemed to be produced by mass irrational feelings. Gothein's concern was more with the second, mass phenomena (*VDG*, 1911: 221–22). He maintained that mass panic often comes with a sense of submitting to some stronger power, that people who are panicking feel they have lost all sense of power, or even will (*VDG*, 1911: 223–24). While this feeling prevails during any mass panic, it is even more pronounced at night – with darkness comes unease at not knowing, a feeling there is something secretive that cannot be comprehended (*VDG*, 1911: 225). This lack of comprehension occurs because panic situations do not build up steadily in readily identifiable stages or steps. However long it takes to build up, the moment of panic always comes with an immediacy that is never expected (*VDG*, 1911: 226). This is apparent when troops flee in panic. Troops can face a vicious onslaught for hours, until suddenly something prompts them to flee in terror (*VDG*, 1911: 227, 230). Because panic among troops destroys the sense of military institution, Gothein declared it the worst type of panic (*VDG*, 1911: 231). Yet he immediately went on to describe numerous other instances of panic that seemed to him just as terrible. We forget, today, that terrorism is not just a recent phenomenon – targeted killings, mass bombings and similar acts took place more than 100 years ago. Gothein described the panic caused by assassinations during the Italian Renaissance, which in his time were mirrored by the panic caused by attacks by anarchists. Today, terrorist acts occur in many parts of the world (*VDG*, 1911: 231).

Gothein pointed to the fact that panic can start among any group of people in the most unexpected places. In the 'City of Enlightenment' – Berlin – there were epidemics of panic among schoolgirls – all for no apparent reason (*VDG*, 1911: 234). When panic breaks out, there is an almost total loss of reason. Gothein used as examples panic generated by fire. When fire breaks out in a theatre, there is mass panic – Gothein offered the view that people are already under suggestion, so the fire 'rips' the people out of a dream and into a horrifying reality. Or, in another real-life example from Heidelberg, Gothein told of a fire in a house that prompted guests in neighbouring hotels to flee the city, with one woman willing to pay almost anything for a car to take her to her husband in Berlin (*VDG*, 1911: 227). As bad as a fire is, Gothein finally maintained that the worst disaster that can result in panic is an earthquake, for the simple reason that an earthquake destroys all that is steady and supporting (*VDG*, 1911: 229).

Horrifying as they are, even plagues did not seem to Gothein to prompt the same degree of panic. Yet his historical account of plagues, beginning with the plague that descended on Athens during the Peloponnesian War, seemed to undermine this claim (*VDG*, 1911: 239). Gothein moved on to discuss the Romans, who, despite being the most disciplined people and having great institutions, were nevertheless prone to occasional bouts of panic (*VDG*, 1911: 241). Frederick the Great and Napoleon, who both looked to Caesar as a hero, saw occasions when their troops fled in panic (*VDG*, 1911: 244).

Gothein concluded with several observations. Of all types of mass phenomena, mass panic is the most worthless and destructive. The roots of mass panic lie in psychology, and Wilhelm Dilthey, Gothein's teacher, unfortunately had not had enough to say about these matters (*VDG*, 1911: 246–47). The efforts of Max Weber to explain important social phenomena had been an immense help. However, social life is so multi-faceted and so complex that it is difficult to comprehend. To explain it is the task of sociology (*VDG*, 1911: 247–48).

No time was set aside for discussion because the next paper was scheduled to be presented. However, time was to be allowed for discussion of Gothein's paper on panic with the discussion following the next paper. Unfortunately, because the paper that followed prompted a lively debate, Gothein's intriguing paper on panic was, in consequence, virtually ignored.

The paper that prompted the debate was entitled 'Wirtschaft und Recht' ('Economy and Justice') and was given by political economist Andreas Voigt. On the face of it, this paper should not have provoked such debate. Voigt did not want to give an exact definition of economy or justice, but to explore the relationship between the two, a connection that was perfectly well understood by most of the audience.

Voigt began by noting that the relationship between the economy and justice is part of the larger problem of the relationship between the economy and social life in general (*VDG*, 1911: 249). He further distinguished between private economy and the public economy. Voigt was concerned with the public economy, and it was here that he began to provoke some discussion, especially from Weber. Voigt insisted that before discussing the relationship between the two, he had to enquire into the essences of economy and justice. For many years, Weber had objected to the notion of essences and particularly the idea that a non-entity might have an 'essence'. Voigt allowed that neither was particularly easy to define, but pointed out that justice was connected to public judgements and public power (*VDG*, 1911: 250). As to economy, people had tried to define it in terms of motives, purposes and means. Voigt said that motives are of two types, egoistic and altruistic, but in fact, most motives are of the first type. There is an economic and so egoistic motive at work even in the production of books, plays and works of art (*VDG*, 1911: 254). Voigt wanted to insist that the economy does not involve only purposes, means or motives, but the relationship between all three (*VDG*, 1911: 255); and, furthermore, that to an economist, the end may not be most important. For example, generals would be interested in the fundamental destruction of an enemy, but an economist would be concerned with the means to be used to accomplish this, in cost of people, materials and time (*VDG*, 1911: 256).

Voigt turned his attention to the notion of justice, putting forward the idea of passive duty, that is, the duty not to hinder someone else; and active duty – duty that must be carried out. Voigt was principally concerned with passive duty, an area in which conflict is common (*VDG*, 1911: 259, 261). Voigt insisted that not all social life is economic life, but that all social life has an economic component. There should therefore be some way of regulating the economic component of social life (*VDG*, 1911: 257). Here, Voigt moved into the sphere of ethics. He acknowledged that economy and justice are not concerned with ethics per se, but that there is a part of ethics that is connected with social policy. And in Voigt's view, all economists since Adam Smith have been concerned with social policy. Furthermore, it is the province of an economist to be concerned with the fairness of, say, the treatment of the modern worker (*VDG*, 1911: 264–65).

Voigt was attacked on two fronts. The Frankfurt jurist Oswalt objected to, among other things, Voigt's so-called 'maximum of success' (*VDG*, 1911: 256, 271). Oswalt rejected the idea of quantification in every instance. While to spend 20 Marks on food or clothing is a quantifiable issue, the decision as to which of the two items the money should be spent on is not an economic/ quantifiable issue (*VDG*, 1911: 271). The second line of attack was an objection to Voigt's having blurred the line between economic and ethical issues. Weber accused Voigt of apparently having blurred the line between the notion of law as an institution made up of laws relating to a range of topics; and the concept of law as a vehicle for prescribing norms. When the law is a vehicle for prescribing norms, it has moved beyond the realm of fact into the realm of value, and that leads immediately to value judgements. It is one thing to allow value judgements when dealing with the law; quite another to allow value judgements when dealing with economic history (*VDG*, 1911: 266–67).

Hermann Kantorowicz also gave a paper that dealt with the sociology of law. Entitled 'Rechtswissenschaft und Soziologie' ('Legal Science and Sociology'), Kantorowicz's paper focused less on law and sociology and their connection with essences; and more on the Neo-Kantian emphasis on knowledge. As evidence of this emphasis, Kantorowicz cited Rickert's Neo-Kantian writings on methodology several times, and also the writings of Emil Lask, Rickert's student, and Weber (*VDG*, 1911: 280, 295–96, 297, 305). Kantorowicz rejected the idea that the question 'What is sociology?' can be answered and reminded his audience that the speakers who preceded him at the conference had not spoken directly about 'Law', or 'Culture', or anything similar, but had spoken in terms of relationships to these topics (*VDG*, 1911: 277–78). Speaking about law specifically, Kantorowicz objected to the idea that judges simply apply the law in such a way that a machine could do it (*VDG*, 1911: 279, see also 303). Instead, the judge must consider various aspects of the case and select the relevant law(s) to apply to the appropriate fact(s). In discussing this process of selection, Kantorowicz drew frequently on Rickert's writings on methodology (*VDG*, 1911: 280, 295–97, 305).

In his comments on Kantorowicz's paper, Weber agreed that law is not the mere application of law to facts, but rather the interpretation of laws in relation to the facts (*VDG*, 1911: 324–25). In his response to Voigt, Weber objected to the idea that a 'scientist' can observe all facts as if he were an omniscient god (*VDG*, 1911: 329). In his most caustic spirit, Weber found it almost unbeliev-able that the most 'value-free' paper of the conference came from a *theologian* (meaning Troeltsch); and that only with a theologian was it possible to discuss issues without resorting to making value judgements (*VDG*, 1911: 323–24). What prompted Weber's emphatic response was Gothein's insistence that value judgements about the past not only *cannot be excluded* but *should not be excluded* from a discussion about the legal practices of the past, because they inevitably dealt with norms (*VDG*, 1911: 323). It is necessary to talk of norms in order to speak in terms of progress or regression. To eliminate discussion of value judgements here is to 'castrate' legal history.[17]

Gothein's remarks were met with applause, but Weber's irritation, if not anger, is clearly in evidence in his correspondence. Furthermore, he objected to Goldscheid's remarks to Ploetz's paper on race, in which Goldsheid insisted that it is not possible to speak of a process of selection except in value terms. To discuss the notion of the 'fittest' is to imply a level of values; and to speak of some natural goal is also to imply value judgements (*VDG*, 1911: 141–43). In a letter to Franz Eulenburg from 27 October, Weber gave a quick summary of his opinion: Voigt's paper was factually solid, but not as good as it might have been, partly because Voigt's wife had died only eight days before the conference. Ploetz's paper was the usual unclarified 'pan-biology', Gothein's was 'superficial' and Sombart's was a 'feuilleton' – the review section of a newspaper. Troeltsch's paper was outstanding, above all it was value-free and the debate was the best of the day. Kantorowicz's paper was 'very good' but the discussion was 'scandalous'. This stemmed from three sources: the discussion of the D.G.S. statute prohibiting value judgements was 'silly'; Tönnies' 'schoolmasterish' insertion of comments; and the protest that was generated (Weber, 1994: 655).

On the same day (27 October), Weber wrote to the Board of Directors of the D.G.S. and complained about the conduct of the session's chairperson (meaning Tönnies) and the uproar over value-free enquiry. Again, he announced his intention to resign from the Board of Directors, effective from 1 January 1911.[18] He was resigning out of a sense of frustration and because he thought there needed to be a jurist on the Board (Weber, 1994: 669). Weber

17 *VDG*, 1911: 323. In their article 'Max Weber as Legal Historian' Harold J. Berman and Charles J. Reid, Jr. claim that Weber was not a 'legal historian'. Weber was either 'unhistorical' in his analyses of legal systems, or he neglected legal history in his discussions. In their view, Weber never appreciated the role of law in the 'revolutionary formation and gradual evolution of the Western City' (Berman and Reid, 2000: 231, 233).

18 Weber, 1994: 659–61. There seems to be some confusion about the reference – Weber had complained about Goldscheid's behaviour and in the Note to Weber's letter to the Board of Directors of 27 October, the reference is given to Goldscheid in connection to Kantorowicz's paper (Weber, 1994: 665 and 660, Note, 1). However, Goldscheid does not comment on Kantorowicz's paper but Gothein does and in his response to Kantorowicz Weber specifically refers to Gothein's comments immediately preceding (*VDG*, 1911: 322, 327). The answer is that Goldscheid had requested that his comments on Kantorowicz's paper not be printed, to which Weber agreed (Weber, 1998: 210 and Note 1, 219).

continued to work hard for the D.G.S., providing a proposal for the statutes for a sub-group on statistics, working to secure a publisher for the Proceedings (Paul Siebeck) and ensuring that the minutiae were correctly transmitted to him. (Weber, 1994: 708–09 and Weber, 1998: 80, 123–25, 128–29, 215–17). Pressing personal legal problems prevented him from submitting a timely report to the Board meeting of October 1911. And by March 1912 he had offered the theme of 'nationality' for the forthcoming second conference (Weber, 1998: 447, 448, 483–84).

The D.G.S. from 1912 until 1930

The first conference set the tone and substance for the following decades of conferences. It is instructive to see in the reports of subsequent conferences, from 1912, how the D.G.S. perpetuated its methods and how it chose the themes for the conferences. This is also helpful because it shows how sociology came to be regarded as a science and how it became institutionalized. I conclude with the 1930 conference for two reasons. First, by then, the D.G.S. had 'won its struggle to be recognized as an independent science' (Geiger, 1931: 568). Second, that was the last conference until after the Second World War.

The second conference took place in Berlin, between 20 and 22 October 1912. The D.G.S. decided to limit the printed comments to the second conference, perhaps because of Goldscheid's comments of the first conference and the problems they had caused. An additional reason could have been the tone of some of the comments about the main topic: nationality (*VDG*, 1913: V).

The opening address was not, however, on nationality, but on culture, and it deserves comment here for a number of reasons. First, it was given by Alfred Weber and it contains similarities to but also contrasts with the work of his brother, Max Weber.[19] Like Max, Alfred demonstrates a mastery of a wide range of concrete and theoretical materials; unlike Max, Alfred had a philosophical, if not poetic, feel for his topic. Second, some of the points that Alfred made here in 'Der soziologische Kulturbegriff' ('The Sociological Concept of Culture') he also made in his contribution to 'Kultursoziologie' in Alfred Vierkandt's *Handwörterbuch der Soziologie*, which was published almost 20 years later. Third, Alfred made some intriguing comments about the human condition.

---

19 I use Alfred Weber's first name to help ensure that there is no confusion between the two brothers. I do not do so out of lack of respect. If anything, his paper and other works underscore his importance and the fact that his work is often overlooked in favour of that of his famous older brother.

Alfred Weber began by noting that there has long been a tendency to derive the human condition from one single, central notion. This is true of St Augustine, with his idea of the *civitas dei* in the natural world. It is true of Hegel, with his concept of God-willed progress in the consciousness of freedom; and it is true of many others (*VDG*, 1913: 1). These attempts to derive the human condition from a single idea are doomed to fail for the simple reason that humans find themselves in two different 'worlds' (*VDG*, 1913: 3–4): the physical world and the spiritual world – the world of biology and the world of culture (*VDG*, 1913: 9–10). The experiences of the physical world make us think that there is some natural progression in the spiritual world as well, but that is not and cannot be the case (*VDG*, 1913: 11–14, see also Weber, 1931: 290). Alfred allowed that there is a sense of dualism, of a subject and an object, which was captured so well by Descartes (*VDG*, 1913: 19–20). Alfred also allowed that the 'subjective' and spiritual part becomes 'objectified' in such cultural phenomena as the state, the law, the economy and other social super-structural forms (*VDG*, 1913: 17). He warned against construing these as a system of empty mechanics; consideration of any word written by Shakespeare or of any body painted by Michelangelo should dispel that conception (*VDG*, 1931: 19). From these observations, Alfred concluded that, through culture, we are able to create a new world (*VDG*, 1913: 20).

Paul Barth, philosopher and sociologist, offered a discussion of the genetic aspects of nationality in his 'Die Nationalität in ihrer soziologischen Bedeutung' ('Nationality in its Sociological Significance'). He began by sketching three natural drives that unite to form a drive to 'nationalism'. They are: the social impulse; the drive to procreate; and the parental drive to protect and raise their offspring (*VDG*, 1913: 21–22). By this, Barth is not claiming that there is any inherent specific biological drive to form a nation. He says that the idea of 'nation' is foreign to Homer and is first represented by Antigone's conflict with the 'state'; it is also found in Apollo's care for the Greeks (*VDG*, 1913: 25, 27–28). The Greek notion of *paideia* should not lead us to think that the Greeks were non-national.[20] In a similar vein, Barth noted that Germans such as Schiller, Herder and Goethe held humanitarian ideals, as well as national ones. While he offered quotations from all three in which they denounce nationalist sentiments, he also pointed to passages in which they exalt Germany's greatness (*VDG*, 1913: 37–39). The high point is reached with Fichte's national ideal (*VDG*, 1913: 39–41).

Up to this point, Barth tried to giving a historical account, but he turned

---

20 *Paideia* is difficult to translate. It means 'education' in a full sense. encompassing mental, spiritual and even physical 'education'. Barth uses it here in the sense of humanity (*VDG*, 1913: 34).

briefly to a sociological one. Kant's 'Good Will' and Fichte's 'nation' are both sociological ideals, the ideals of free people (*VDG*, 1913: 45). Echoing Alfred Weber's final remarks, Barth concluded with the observation that a *Volk*, a 'nation' is not merely some physical 'entity' but is also a 'spiritual' one (*VDG*, 1913: 48).

As expected, Barth's paper generated a fair amount of debate. Ludo Moritz Hartmann suggested that nationality was bound up with culture and the destiny of peoples, while Alfred offered that it is not simple to specify what a 'nation' is, for there are many elements that seem to come into play, including language, territory and so on (*VDG*, 1913: 49–51, 53). Later, Alfred took up Hartmann's notion of nationality and culture and wondered about the effects literature had upon it (*VDG*, 1913: 72–73). A Dr Böttger objected to the fact that Alfred minimized the effect of national music. Robert Michels reminded the audience that many songs have trans-national significance, and gave the Marseillaise as an example. Tönnies recalled the multiplicity of senses of the term 'nationality' and remarked that Böttger was using it in a very modern way. Barth repeated his point about the idea of nationality and its power-seeking connotations; and Alfred Weber again emphasized the multiple senses of the word (*VDG*, 1913: 73–74).

A number of points that overlapped between Ludo Moritz Hartmann's 'Die Nation als politischer Faktor' ('The Nation as Political Factor') and Robert Michels' 'Die historische Entwicklung des Vaterslandsgedankens' ('The Historical Development of the Notion of the Fatherland'). Both scholars agreed that the concept of the nation was a relatively recent phenomenon; that culture and language played large roles in its formation; and that the notion was difficult to define. Whereas Hartmann looked to the east and the south to see how the concept of nation could be both construed and opposed (he had in mind the problem areas between the German–Slavic and German–Italian regions), Michels took a broader approach historically, politically and theoretically. Specifically, Michels observed that the notion of patriotism was found in the British belief in freedom of the early eighteenth century, and in pre- and post-revolutionary France (*VDG*, 1913: 81, 85–86). It took on a different aspect with Napoleon's rise to power. People from different areas of France supported Napoleon, but so did many people from other countries. Michels indicated that with the exception of Prussia, most of the German areas happily welcomed Napoleon and served on his side (*VDG*, 1913: 159–60). This led Michels to declare that the notions of nationality and Fatherland are far more complex and far less compelling than many scholars think. In particular, Marxist followers disavow the notion of Fatherland and are both anti-patriotic and anti-military (*VDG*, 1913: 165–74). Michels also argues that the notion of an inborn allegiance to one's homeland is bogus. If a young Eskimo is placed in Rome, he will adopt Italian culture; if a young Italian is placed in Greenland, he will adopt Eskimo culture (*VDG*, 1913: 176).

Michels concluded by saying that it is impossible to pinpoint a time for the development of the notion of the Fatherland and that it can be construed in many ways – as a state, a race, a language, or any combination of these. He emphasized that the development of such a notion is not any indication of moral progress, but of a historically necessary development (*VDG*, 1913: 181–84).

It is surprising that neither of these speeches generated much discussion. Instead, discussion centred on an unclear and badly thought-out speech on race, in which the author, Franz Oppenheimer, was roundly criticized (*VDG*, 1913: 185, 186–87). In particular, Max Weber challenged Oppenheimer's theory of racial progress by pointing to the decline of the Roman Empire (*VDG*, 1913: 188–89).

In the Treasurer's report, Weber presented the membership figures: now at 334. Tönnies, Simmel and Sombart were re-elected to the Chair: Sombart took over Weber's job when Weber and Vierkandt resigned. In a letter to the leader, Hermann Beck, Weber gave as his reason the battle of value judgements. He wished the Society all the best, but wrote that he would no longer attend any of its conferences (Weber, 1998: 709). He need not have been concerned about attending any more D.G.S. conferences. Weber died two years prior to the next conference.

The third D.G.S. conference did not take place until 1922, ten years after the second. It was held in Jena on 24 and 25 September. There were many reasons for the long gap, of which very few had to do with sociology proper, and most stemmed from personal or financial factors.

In his Presidential Opening Address, Tönnies noted that the intention was to hold a conference every two years. The second took place in 1912, so the third was originally planned for 1914. (*VDG*, 1923: 1). However, the outcome of the war for Germany, Austria and, indeed, the whole cultural world was nothing less than catastrophic. There was no need for Tönnies to go into any detail: for those present, the memories were all too evident and painful. There were revolutions all over Germany; the Weimar Republic was founded, but on rather shaky grounds. The Austro-Hungarian Empire collapsed after a 600-year history. There was widespread hunger and staggering inflation. An attempt to renew the Society conference in 1919 foundered. A letter was sent out, but it generated only a slight response. Many of the intended recipients had apparently moved and left no forwarding address and many had died. Tönnies mentioned the names of many of those who had passed away. Of the original five, Simmel and Weber had died and Troeltsch was to follow in early 1923.

Tönnies recounted how in 1920 he started to plan again for the conference (*VDG* 1923: 2).

Compared with the first two conferences, the attendance at the third was small – nine people only (Käsler, 1984: 606). And unlike the previous two, this conference was devoted to one theme: revolution. Only two papers were given. Leopold von Wiese gave one on the possibility of establishing a *sociology* of revolution, in which he noted that historians had provided most of the writings on revolution, whereas sociologists had mostly ignored the notion (*VDG*, 1923: 7). Von Wiese stressed that, as a sociologist, he would refrain from passing ethical judgement on specific revolutions. He vigorously rejected the question of guilt for any particular revolution as unsociological (*VDG*, 1923: 9); and he objected to utopian hopes for the success of any revolution. As in war, the gains from the change of regime need to be weighed against the number of probable victims. Von Weise ended on a rather pessimistic note – that revolutions are more like strong currents and violently swirling water, and so are more suited to metaphysical speculation than to scientific investigation (*VDG*, 1923: 22–23). With this, von Weise did not intend to minimize revolutionary fervour. Instead, he suggested that the way for a state to deal with it is not to allow the conditions to fester that generate the need and desire for revolutionary change.

The second paper continued the same theme. In 'Zur Soziologie der Revolution' ('On the Sociology of Revolution'), Ludo Moritz Hartmann defined revolution as the radical change of power. He also insisted that a 'legitimate' revolution is as much a contradiction in terms as the perpetual legal continuity of a state is also a fiction (*VDG*, 1923: 25). A revolution occurs when a change of power is brought about by a mass movement of human beings; and revolution is only a continuation of evolution by other, more radical, means (*VDG*, 1923: 26–27). Hartmann focused mainly on the modern workers' revolutions, although he took up the issue of other revolutions. While he acknowledged that revolutionary activity can be an outlet for hysterical impulses; he also noted that like other historical phenomena it is something that can be sociologically investigated (*VDG*, 1923: 37–39).

The debate began the next day and was noteworthy for three points only. One commentator complained that since revolutions were so atypical, it seemed strange to try to discuss a single 'type' of revolution. Furthermore, to discuss whether a certain revolution was worthwhile is not a scientific question but an ethical one, one that rather leads in the direction of Marx. The third point was that sociological investigations should move away from Marxist value judgements and towards the value-free sociological investigations of Weber and Troeltsch (*VDG*, 1923: 41–43).

The fourth conference was held in Heidelberg between 29 and 30 September 1924. The number of people in attendance had more than doubled. They included such familiar figures as Tönnies, Sombart, Alfred Weber and Robert Michels. Tönnies began by speaking about those important members who had died during the past two years. Of the six, he included Troeltsch and Paul Natorp. Tönnies reminded his audience of the important work that Troeltsch had done for the sociology of religion and in this way, purposely linked him to Weber. Natorp is best remembered as one of the last leading figures of the Marburg school of Neo-Kantianism, but Tönnies mentioned his work on social life – education and support – and in this sense counted him as a sociologist.

Tönnies then turned the platform over to Alfred Weber. As Deacon of the Faculty of Philosophy and a citizen of Heidelberg, Alfred Weber welcomed the audience to the city and spoke of the Heidelberg tradition of enquiry. Of the four papers given, two were devoted to the important enquiry into science and social structure.

The Austrian Marxist, Max Adler, gave the second paper, in which he noted his major agreements with the first paper. Where he differed, which was primarily on Marxist grounds, he received mainly negative reactions. His main intention was to combine Kantian critical epistemology with Marxist historical-dialectical materialism to form a 'modern critical sociology'. To his audience, this seemed virtually impossible (*VDG*, 1925: 212; see also 217, 221, 227).

By contrast, most of the responses to the paper by the philosopher-social thinker Max Scheler were positive. The audience approved his presentation of three major historical types of epochs – theological, metaphysical and positivist. In fact, these were basically taken over from Comte, but Scheler emphasized the dependence of scientific enquiry on social forms (see *VDG*, 1925: 217). Considering the first, theological type, Scheler observed that for the Catholic Church, the search for knowledge is not a major concern: the search for knowledge about God is most important. As he put it, those who see the stars as manifestations of God are not yet ready for a science of astronomy (see *VDG*, 1925: 127–30). Scheler's second type, the metaphysical, does not fare much better. Because it is almost always a spiritual elitist, this type cares little for the inductive and deductive results of positive science and prefers a priori speculation regarding some Absolute (*VDG*, 1925: 135, 142). Scheler notes that by the time of Luther and Descartes, there was a dualism between meta-physical and scientific interests (*VDG*, 1925: 150). The third type, positivist, rejects all theological and metaphysical concerns as well as limitations and wishes to deal strictly with empirically verifiable situations. Scheler points to the positivist's concern with content but also notes a rising interest in form. He ends on the note that with secularization and the maturing of positivism, the way for a metaphysics of nature and humans is now open (*VDG*, 1925: 180, 219). However, Scheler does not hint as to how such a metaphysics can arise.

The fifth conference was held in Vienna between 26 and 29 September 1926 and drew 26 participants. Many were familiar from the early years of the D.G.S., but with the increase in participants, changes were needed and were accordingly made. There were now sub-groups on methodology, relationships and other subjects. The two main papers were on the issue of democracy. In his written introduction, Leopold von Wiese noted that political issues, especially regarding the value of democracy, drew particularly passionate responses and provoked quick judgements (*VDG*, 1927: VI).

Tönnies gave the first of the two papers. Although he mostly steered away from making passionate judgements, it was clear that he experienced the notion of freedom as a passionate concern; and saw the love of freedom and the pride of the free person as ethical concerns (*VDG*, 1927: 19). Democracy also meant the furthering of Christian ideals, including brotherliness, the diminishing of the suffering of the poor and the emancipation of women (*VDG*, 1927: 21). Although democracy implies ethical ideals, Tönnies noted that the essential character of the modern state is its impersonal rationality, and this implies the separation of the state, dominated as it is by rationality, from the church, which is dominated by authority (*VDG*, 1927: 28–30). In his closing remarks, Tönnies turned from his 'scientific' discussion to his 'ethical' instruction: only with fundamental and far-reaching economic reforms in social life is there any real hope of democracy surviving (*VDG*, 1927: 36).

The other paper on democracy was given by Hans Kelsen. Kelsen was trained in the law and held positions as a professor in Vienna and as a member of the Constitutional Court. From his earliest works, Kelsen made it clear that, like Weber, he rejected the conflating of 'is' and 'ought', so in his paper he refrained from the imperatives that characterized Tönnies' paper.[21] Kelsen acknowledged that there is a dualism between 'is' and 'ought', which he characterizes as the dualism between ideology and reality (*VDG*, 1927: 39). He noted that when it comes to the study of human institutions, an 'ideal' often creeps into the most 'scientific' of investigations. As he put it, a plant cannot speak up and maintain that it is really an animal or a mineral, but any state can insist that it is really 'democratic' (*VDG*, 1927: 41; see also 66).

Kelsen believed democracy to be intimately connected to two issues. On the first – parliamentarianism – he maintained that democracy is possible only in connection with a parliament. On the second – selecting leaders – he believed

21 Kelsen had been made a member of the Advisory Committee of the D.G.S. in 1922, see *VDG*, 1923: 56. His fact–value distinction is evident in most all of his works, beginning in 1920.

that the democratic ideal of a leaderless democracy can never be realized (*VDG*, 1927: 44, 55). There must, therefore, be some process of selecting a leader from among the masses, and that, Kelsen maintained, is accomplished through elections (*VDG*, 1927: 57). The question is, once the leader has been elected by the majority, how can the minority keep from being reduced, if not eliminated? This is often accomplished by compromise, and Kelsen insisted that any exchange, including a contract, is, in fact, a compromise (*VDG*, 1927: 64). He concluded with the observation that ideology often leads to bloody conflicts with little hope for freedom, whereas democratic parliamentarianism most often leads to the realization of peace (*VDG*, 1927: 68).

Thirty people participated in the sixth conference, which was held between 17 and 19 September 1928 in Zürich. Again, some of the names were familiar from before – Tönnies, Sombart and von Wiese, but also Franz Oppenheimer, Karl Mannheim and Paul Honigsheim. Oppenheimer held the first Chair of Sociology at Frankfurt, Mannheim became famous for his work on ideology and Honigsheim was to make a name for himself in legal sociology; both had studied at Heidelberg under Max Weber.

The seventh conference was held in Berlin between 28 September and 1 October 1930. By this time, the D.G.S. was very much an institution. It had received the respect it had long sought (Käsler, 1984: 470). Almost 40 people took part and there were sub-groups on art, sociography, political sociology, methodology and other topics. The main theme, to which two papers were devoted, was the press and public. Commentators included Tönnies but also Erich Voegelin, who later, in 1939, would have to leave Germany and Austria for political reasons; and Carl Schmitt, who later became the leading legal theoretician for the Nazi Party.

Concluding Remarks

In his written Preface to the proceedings of 1930, von Wiese looked back over the 20-year history of the D.G.S. and its conferences. He noted the increase in participation and the broadening of the themes. He reminded his readers of the 1912 conference, at which Max Weber fought so hard for value-free judgements; of the 1930 conference, where the main topic of the press was originally Weber's idea (*VDG*, 1931: IX–X). Von Wiese was justified in his pleasant recollections of the D.G.S.'s past and of its present condition.

Yet in a few short years, the D.G.S. would be virtually disbanded because of the Nazi rise to power. Many sociologists were forced to retire.[22] These

22 Lepsius says that of the approximately 150 members of the D.G.S. as of July 1929 only 50 can be regarded as sociologists. He breaks down the remaining 100 into 50 economists, 13 jurists,

included Alfred Vierkandt, whose *Handwörterbuch der Soziologie* from 1931 is still worth consulting, even today, and Alfred Weber. Many more sociologists were forced to emigrate. These included Hermann Kantorowicz, Hans Kelsen, Paul Honigsheim, Karl Mannheim and Max Horkeimer. Others, including Tönnies, von Wiese, Vierkandt and Alfred Weber, were forced into an internal emigration. M. Rainer Lepsius lists over 180 sociologists and a comparable number of political scientists who had to leave Germany because of the Nazis. These included the philosophers Theodor Adorno, Herbert Marcuse and Leo Strauss; the religious thinkers Paul Tillich and Martin Buber; the economists Joseph Schumpeter and Hans Morgenthau; the psycho-analyst Erich Fromm; the political thinker Hannah Arendt; and the educator Bruno Bettelheim (Lepsius, 1981: 487–500). Very few of the early members of the D.G.S. had any Nazi sympathies (see Käsler, 1984: 525–29). Many of them were left-leaning and most of them wished for some kind of real demo-cracy. Their sociological studies of politics and power provided little incentive to be sympathetic to Nazi principles and practices.

The founding of the Deutsche Gesellschaft für Soziologie was a momentous occasion for the study of sociology in Germany. Even though Simmel and Tönnies still did not hold full professorships, they were held in high regard. Sombart and even more so Weber and Troeltsch were considered leading lights of German intellectual circles, and their opinions were highly respected. Thus, the inaugural conference was even more important than the founding of the Society, for this was the first public occasion for the D.G.S. The founder members were, despite Weber's opinion, quite successful in separating facts from values, science from opinion. This was especially true of Troeltsch and Sombart and was also true of Simmel and Tönnies. They were therefore justified in believing that what they offered to the public was an indication of sociology as a *science*. Virtually all the founder members were highly opinion-ated and rather left-leaning. Tönnies, Weber and most of the others argued passionately for social justice. They succeeded in reserving those opinions for appropriate places, and the lecture hall and the conference room were not among them. As Weber said about the prophets and demagogues in *Wissen-schaft als Beruf* – they should go out into the streets and speak publicly (Weber, 1992: 97). As professors, intellectual integrity was an obligation. By separating facts from opinions they were better able to earn respect as *sociologists* and thereby for *sociology*.[23] And by setting this stage in this way, they set the stage

---

7 philosophers and the other 30 as historians, psychologists, or not academically active. Lepsius, 1981: 463.

23 There are those who claim that it is impossible to separate facts from values and there are those who claim that it should not be attempted. And, then there are those who claim that these

for the institutionalization of sociology. As we approach the 100 years of the founding of the Deutsche Gesellschaft für Soziologie it may be appropriate to look at what the original members in Frankfurt said at the inaugural conference about the issues, methods and goals of sociology.

---

thinkers often failed to practise what they preached. My own opinion, such as it is, is that one should, one can and that they did. This is not the place to take up these issues, but I should like to point out three things. First, in the 'Objectivität' essay Weber takes pains to explain that while it is extraordinarily difficult to draw the line between statements of ideals and the analysis of facts, the distinction needs to be made clear to everyone, especially to oneself. (Weber, 1922a: 157). Second, in his comment on Sombart's paper he refers to something as *großartig* ('terrific', 'first rate', 'sublime'). He immediately notes that it is a value judgement and immediately retracts it. Third, Weber never sought to minimize the importance of values and value judgements. In fact, because they were so extraordinarily important he sought to keep discussions of them free from mundane jargon and the muddling mixing of them with facts (see Weber, 1926: 423).

The Papers
of the First DGS Conference

GEORG SIMMEL

Sociology of Society[1]

[Wednesday Evening, 19 October 1910
At the invitation of the Frankfurt Academy for Social and Trade Sciences,
Professor Dr Georg Simmel, Berlin, gave the following lecture on 'Sociology
of Society' at the Greeting Evening, Wednesday 19 October.]

In the old argument about the essence of society, there is the view that there is
a mystic significance in the idea that all human life drinks first and equally with
reality; and there is the view that the essence of society should be only an
abstract concept that the observer of the reality of the single existence can
grasp afterwards, much as trees and streams, houses and fields are perceived as
'a landscape'. The Society must concede that in fact this argument has a
double meaning. On the one hand, in their immediate sensory existences as
carriers of the socializing process, individuals join together to become the
higher unity that is called 'a society'. On the other hand, there are the interests
that motivate living individuals to come together – economic and ideal interests,

1 All of the papers in this volume are difficult to translate but Simmel's paper is perhaps the
most difficult. Many of the problems stem from his abstractness – his discussions of social
interactions are often in terminology that renders his meaning opaque. One thing to keep in mind
is that he is continuing the Kantian division between form and content – like Kant, his interest is in
the first. When Simmel uses 'pure', it is as in 'form' – without content. A second point: like Kant,
he is interested in dynamics, specifically social dynamics. A third point is his notion of opposing
states or conditions, hence his repeated use of *Wechselwirkung*. Fourth, Simmel examines social
relations that tend to be small, such as the flirting interaction between a man and a woman, and he
discusses social interaction that seems insignificant, such as small talk, jokes, and the like. These
notions seem almost trivial in contrast with the great themes of the other papers: Tönnies' on the
essence of sociology, Weber's on the nature of newspapers, or Sombart's on technology and
culture. Yet, it is Simmel's point that because of its *apparent* lack of importance sociological
analysis is warranted. Finally, in 1910 Simmel had not developed his *Lebensphilosophie* that became
the major philosophy of his final years but he was moving in that direction: hence his
preoccupation with the notion of 'life'.

combative and erotic, religious and 'caritative' (*sic*).[2] In order to satisfy such drives,[3] in order to achieve such goals, the immense, manifold forms of social life grow. They all grow with one another, for one another, in one another, against one another, and through one another, in state and community, in church and economic union, in family and associations. Just as energy effects appear from material elements to bring the material into form, so that from innumerable 'things' there are human impulses and interests that move us and force us towards others in the forms of unification. Thus, we go from a mere number of co-existing beings to the enduring essence that is a 'society'.

Within this process, or outside it, there now develops a particular socio-logical form corresponding to art and play,[4] which draws its form out and leaves its reality behind. It remains here, if the concept of the drive to play or the drive to art possesses a real explanatory value; in any case, it indicates that each single game or artistic activity contains a non-effected universal, which differs from it in content or form. A certain equality of satisfaction lies in the gymnastic performance and in the card game, or also in the music or the sculpture, which has nothing to do with what is special about the music or the sculpture, but only with the fact that each of the two are art or each of those is first a game. A common, equal psychic reaction and psychic need binds all these and differs from the special interests that are peculiar to their differences. It is possible to speak in the same sense of the *social drive* of humanity. It is certainly as a result of special needs and interests that people band together into an economic union or a band of blood brothers, into a cult of contem-poraries or a band of robbers. Beyond these special contents, all these societies emanate from one feeling. It comes from the satisfaction that accompanies socialization, when the loneliness of the individual is lifted, and the result is unification with others. Certainly, in individual cases this feeling can arise through psychic counter-instances – the form of the society can be perceived as a simple, accursed need for our specific purposes. Yet, typically, a feeling for the value of social formation is interwoven into all real initiatives towards social formation. This is a drive that comes from the form of existence and often calls first to its side the real content that individual socialization carries. And just as what I call the artistic drive simultaneously draws out the form from the entirety of apparent things into a specific thing, this drive produces the corresponding form, and the social drive simultaneously draws out the realities

2 The word means 'caring for the soul', but Simmel may have misspoken here. The previous pairings were oppositions; the opposite to 'religious' would be 'secular'.

3 *Trieben*, singular *Trieb*. Simmel uses this word throughout: 'catalyst' or 'force' or 'growth'.

4 Simmel uses the term *Spiel* which can be rendered 'play' or 'game'. I have chosen one or the other based upon the context.

of social life. The form of being with one another, the simple social process that is valuable and good is fully effective, and with it is constituted what we call society in a narrow sense. It is no mere accident of speech that all sociability – (the entirely naturalistic one that should somehow have sense and existence) – places such great value on *form*, on good form. For, form is the reciprocating self-determination, or interaction (*Wechselwirkung*)[5] of the elements from which unity is built. And so for sociability comes the concrete purpose-setting of life, with the connected motivations of socialization that now fall away, so form must accentuate even more strongly and more effectively the so-called free-soaring, reciprocating connections of individuals.

And what art binds with play, the analogy emerges with both in sociability. The given reality of life removes from the game its great formal motive: the hunt and ill-gotten gains, the testing of physical and spiritual power, the contest and the hunt for opportunity, and the favourableness of the powers of life that cannot be influenced. From the material, [it] unburdens and expresses [itself] through the movements of the serious things of life; the game wins its pleasure, but it also wins the symbolic significance that differentiates it from mere pleasure. And even this reveals itself as the essence of society, builds *its* body out of the innumerable fundamental forms of serious relations among humans, for which the level of resistance when rubbing [friction] against reality (*Reibungswiderstände*) is reduced. But from its relationship with form, society wins its sociability, and the more complete it is as sociability. For deeper human beings, sociability has a playful fullness of life and a significance that a superficial rationalism always seeks only in concrete *contents*, so it does not find it here, and so it knows sociability only as a hollow foolishness. Thus, it is equivalent to the scholar who, when faced with a work of art, asks *Qu'est-ce que cela prouve?* ('What does it prove?'). It is not insignificant that in most, perhaps in all European languages, society simply signifies the social act of being together (*geselliges Zusammensein*). The state, the economic society that hangs together by means of some purposeful thoughts (*Zweckgedanken*) is still a 'society' through and through. However, that which is social can even be 'a society' without further addition, because it presents the principle over and above any specific content of any raised form of all that characterized one-sided 'societies'. In an equally abstract manner, all contents are presented in the mere play of the dissolving picture.

From the sociological categories here employed, I therefore designate sociability as the *playform of creating society* (*Spielform der Vergesellschaftung*) and

---

5 Simmel uses this term and variations throughout this paper. *Wechsel* is 'change' as when he uses it below in *wechselnden Daseins* ('changing existence' or 'being'). More often he combines *Wechsel* with *Wirkung* ('effect') to mean 'interaction'.

– *mutatis mutandis* – pertaining to the content-determined concreteness, as an artwork is to reality. What comes first is the great, perhaps the greatest problem for society within sociability to have in its possible solution: how to come up with the measurement of the significance and accentuate the individual in and against the social circle. Insofar as sociability in its pure formations has no real purpose, no content and no result, so to speak, outside the social moment, it rests entirely on personalities. Nothing but satisfaction with this moment – at most with a resonance from it – shall be reached, and so remain the predecessor of its conditions, that in its production is limited to its personal characteristics; the personal properties of amiability, education, cordiality, appeal of every type, are decisive over the character of sociable social settings. However, exactly because all is based upon personalities, the personalities are not allowed to be emphasized, as they are too individual.[6] The cooperation or collision of real interests determines the social form, so that the individual, with his peculiarities, does not present himself in an all-too-unlimited and autonomous way.

But where this conditionality falls away, another form of sociability must occur, to reduce the personal autocracy of the individual in order to make social interaction in general possible. Therefore, in society the feeling of tact (*Taktgefühl*) has such a special significance because the self-regulation of the individual leads to relations with another person, in which no external or immediate egoistical interests override the regulative. And perhaps it is the task of discretion to draw the limits of individual impulsiveness, the accentuations of the 'I', the spiritual and outer demands that serve to further the rights of others. From here comes a very remarkable sociological structure. Nothing has entered into the sociability possessed by the personality as something of an objective significance, by the centre outside the circle. Wealth and social position, education and fame, exceptional capabilities and the personal merit of the individual have no role to play in sociability. At the most, a slight nuance of any immateriality may be permitted to project with reality in general on the art of sociability. Even so, since this objective is bound with the personality, the purest and deepest of that which is personal must be cut out of its function as the element of sociability: that most personal of life, character, temperament, destiny, equally have no place in the framework of sociability. It is tactless to bring into sociability the merely personal humour and irritation, excitement and depression, lightness and darkness of deepest life. Where a socially initiated unification – and not merely one that is superficially societal and conventional – finally centres on individual values, it loses its particular sociability. It comes

6 Simmel seems to suggest here that a social shift from the emphasis on the individual personalities to the individual interests comes because of the personalness of the former.

to an *essence* of a specific social setting, not different from a social or a church meeting in which, for those coming together, the exchange and talk are only the vehicles for some other purpose; while for sociability, these forms are determined in the whole sense and essence of sociological experience. This exclusion of the personal reaches into outward behaviour: a lady would not like to appear as provocative in an intimate, friendly social setting with one or a few men as she would in a larger gathering, where she would be unembarrassed. She feels that she is not engaged as an individual to the extent that she is in the intimate setting and therefore, beneath the impersonal freedom of a mask, can surrender herself there as if she were being herself – but not entirely as she is by herself, rather as an element in a formal meeting.

Man as a whole is still an unformed complex of contents, forces, possibilities and, accordingly, motivations and relations of a changing existence (*wechselnden Daseins*). This reforms itself into a differentiated, limited, determined form. As an economic and a political person, as a family member and as a representative of a profession, he is, so to speak, an ad hoc elaboration of his life material, constructed from a special idea and produced in a special form, a form of life relatively independent from the common and immediate, but not stored in the designated power source of the 'I'. In this sense, man as a social creature is original and individualistic; he does not exhibit this form in any other relationship. On the one hand he has disposed of all the meanings of personality and with only the capacities, fascinations and interests in his humanity, enters into the form of sociability. On the other hand, this form is entirely and thoroughly subjective, and sustains the inward-directedness of the personality. Discretion, which is the first requirement of sociability when opposing others, is yet a requirement in opposing one's own 'I', because in both cases the sociological art form of sociability, if breached, is permitted to degenerate into a sociological naturalism.[7] Therefore, it is possible to speak of individuals being 'above' or 'below' a 'threshold of sociability' (*Geselligkeitsschwelle*). The individual restrainedly enters both in the moment of this social setting, and of the other, where the absolute personal and subjective are combined, to place an objective essence and purpose; the sociability is then no longer central and forming; but, at the most, the formalistic and externally supplied principle.

To this negative determination of the essence of sociability (*Geselligkeits-wesens*), it may be possible to find the positive formal aspect. Kant made it a principle of right that for any group that has a measure of freedom, that freedom can be maintained through the freedom of 'the Other'. If the drive

7 Simmel seems to be suggesting that in social settings one is not confronting just other people, but is also confronting one's self. One needs to control one's one urges in order to prevent what Simmel calls 'sociological naturalism'.

(*Trieb*) of sociability is the source or the substance of sociability, then the principle should emerge that everyone should enjoy the same satisfaction from this drive. If, instead of expressing this idea in terms of drives, a principle of sociability were to be formulated, it would be that everyone should *guarantee* to others the maximum sociable values (happiness, relief, liveliness), which should equal the maximum of those values that one *receives* oneself. On the Kantian basis, the right [just] is thoroughly democratic, so this principle shows the democratic structure of all sociability, which each societal stratification must obviously realize for itself, although sociability among members of various social classes is too often contradictory and painful. Yet even among social equals, the democracy of sociability is a *played* thing (*eine gespielte*). Sociability creates, if you will, an ideal sociological world, in which the happiness of the individual is securely tied to the happiness of everyone else. Here, no one can find satisfaction at the cost of another, by contrast with the other life-formations, which go beyond the ethical imperative, but not by excluding its own immediate, inner principles. Yet this world of sociability, the only one where it is possible for a democracy to have an equality of rights without friction, is an *artificial* world. It is built from the essence, so objectively that it has renounced the entire personal-ness of life, its intensity and extensity, in order to produce an entirely pure one, but through no similar material accent of the de-balancing interaction of one another.[8] If we believe that we embrace sociability 'as humans', which we really are, discarding all burdens, craftiness, the idea of too much and too little, from which our picture is composed, we see that our modern life is overburdened with objective essentials and demands. Removed in this way from our social circle, we believe that we return to our natural-personal being. Yet we overlook the fact that the personal expressed here does not appear in its entire special-ness and natural completeness, but with a certain reserve and the stylization of socializing humans. In earlier times, when humans did not yet have so many actual, objective essentials, so that the law of form was more clearly valid than *personal being*, personal conduct in sociability was much more ceremonial, more rigid, and more strictly regulated on a supra-individual level than today. This reduction of the personal in favour of the significant mass conceded homogeneous interaction (*Wechselwirkung*) to other individuals, swung to the opposite extreme: a specific behaviour in sociability is courtesy, but those having superior force, not only when compared

---

8 On the face of it, this sentence says nothing. However, I think Simmel is trying to say that the world (that is, the social world) is an artificial construct. It is built in such a way that people appear to give up many of their individual wishes and desires in order to have the security of the social world. Consider this in light of what he says below about the social being 'democratic' and the ebb and flow of the social tide.

with the weak, having adopted the attitude that they are more valuable and superior compared to others.[9] If socialization in general is interaction (*Wechsel-wirkung*), it is also equal to the purest and most stylized form, just as symmetry and equilibrium are the most obvious artificial stylized forms of appearance. Insofar as sociability is connected with the character of art or play, there is a complete abstraction of socialization and it demands the purest and the most transparent, as well as the lightest possible form of interaction (*Wechselwirkung*) between equals. It must, in order to will its fundamental idea, fabricate [its] essence, by giving up much of its objective content and modify it both externally as well as internally, so that all are socially equal and each can win social values for himself only under certain circumstances, and so that the others who are interacting (*Wechselwirkenden*) with him can also win. This is a game in which one 'pretends' (*so tut*) that all are equal, as if one especially honoured all others. This is a lie, just as games and art, with all their deviations from reality, are lies.[10] In the moment, just as a painting becomes a lie when it pretends to be reality, practical reality pervades the words and actions of sociability in intentions and happenings. What is inside the autonomous being is right; only in the imminent play of its forms is sociability confirmed, and these will become lies if appearances are no more than an illusion, if social manner belies the reality of goals, so that they are made invisible. This is obviously where the complexity of sociability may easily tempt one to believe that it is real life.

This connection lies close that in sociability what is accommodated and that one can already designate from itself as a sociological play form: above all, that the particular play itself – sociability of all epochs occurs in a wide space. The expression 'society game' (*Gesellschaftsspiel*) is deeply significant, as I have shown. The whole range of interactions or forms of association (*Wechselwirkungs- oder Vergellschaftstungsformen*) between men: the will to outdo and the exchange, the building of political parties and the will to acquire, the change between opposition and co-operation, the outwitting and the revenge – all these come from the purposeful essence of the seriousness of reality, and the game led from a desire for this function and alone supported in life. For even where the game turns on a monetary prize, it is not that, as in many other situations, one can wager; the attraction of this for the right player lies in the dynamic and the opportunity for every sociologically significant display form. The social game has a deeper double meaning: that it is not only played in a society as an external carrier, but is 'played' with, in the 'society'. Furthermore, in the

9 Simmel uses the French term *courtoisie* to stress the connection with the French Courts.

10 The use of terms such as 'pretend' and 'lies' may suggest that Simmel is deprecating social relations, but I think that he is simply trying to describe them.

sociology of gender the erotic exhibits its game form: *coquetry*, which, within sociability finds its lightest, most playful, but also its widest realization. The erotic question between the genders turns on the granting and the denying (the objects of which are naturally infinitely varied and by no means only more radical or even physiological). So, it is the essence of female coquetry that the tension should change back and forth between an indicated granting and an indicated refusal, without letting it come to a decision to reject, without taking all hope from the man. The coquette places her allure on the highest level, so that she can grant the man something that she does not entirely withdraw, without allowing the matter to become serious, swinging ceaselessly between yes and no. She shows her coquettishness equally in the playfulness of the simple and pure form of erotic decisions and can display polar opposites in her wholly unified behaviour. The deciding and decisive essence of both parties has no part in coquetry, and this unburdening of all the weight of firm essence and lasting realities gives coquetry the character of something suspended, distant, ideal. As a result, coquetry can with a certain justification be described as an 'art' and its practitioners 'artists' of coquetry.

However, a natural growth can take place on the basis of sociability, as experience shows, and this must be met with an entirely special behaviour on the part of the man: the man may refuse the allure of the coquetry; or, conversely, so long as he is obviously the victim, he has unwillingly been dragged along from the vibrating half 'yes', half 'no', coquetry has not yet taken on an acceptable form in sociability. It lacks the free interaction (*Wechselwirkung*) and the equivalence of the elements that is the fundamental law of sociability. This first occurs when the man desires nothing more than this balancing act, and puts in a suggestion of something like a distant erotic symbol, and when he no longer reads desire or apprehension into the situation. Coquetry, as it is currently unfolding its charm on the heights of social culture, contains the reality of erotic desire, but has left reality behind and has come out in changing forms (*Wechselspiele*, literally 'change plays') like shadow pictures of seriousness. Where these last enter or stand behind is the entire experience, so to speak. It will become a private concern of both persons at the level of reality but under the sociological signs of sociability. Coquetry is teasing or ironic play, into which the full life of the binding centrality of people in general does not enter, and through which the erotic is released from the material or wholly individual essence to the pure schemata of its interactions (*Wechselwirkungen*). As sociability plays the forms of society, coquetry plays the forms of the erotic – an essential relationship that in the certain measure of each predetermines the element.

The extent to which sociability draws abstractions through its essence is its most significant sociological forms of interaction (*Wechselwirkungsformen*). It now circles itself, providing a shadow, which reveals itself in the broadest carrier of all human communication, in *conversation*. What is decisive here is expressed as an entirely banal experience: humans in all seriousness will talk in order to communicate or inform, but in sociability, talk provides its own rationale; social talking is an indispensable carrier of charm as the living exchange (*Wechseltausch*) of conversation unfolds. All the forms with which this exchange is realized: the argument and the call to recognized norms; the conclusion of peace through compromise; the discovery of common convictions; the thankful acceptance of the new and the rejection of that on which there is no hope of an agreement – each of these forms of communicative interaction (*Wechselwirkung*) has its own meaning, usually in the service of innumerable essences and purposes of human interaction, and that means that in the tension of the game of relations between individuals, they bind and loosen, win and lose, give and take. It is here that the double sense of 'self-conversation' (*sich-Unterhaltens*) comes into its own. So that this game can maintain satisfaction through mere form, the content is not permitted to have its own weight: as soon as the conversation becomes objective (*sachlich*), it is no longer social. It spins on its teleological tip as soon as it elicits a truth that can thoroughly structure its content and so become its purpose. With that, it destroys its character as social conversation, as it does in the face of a serious argument. The *form* of the common seeking of the correct, the *form* of the argument may exist, but that can hardly allow the contents to prevail, just as a picture drawn in perspective would not allow a piece of three-dimensional reality to be integrated into it. It is not as if the essence of social conversation is irrelevant, it should be thoroughly interesting, enthralling, even significant – except that it does not create the purpose of the conversation, that it is not valid for objective results, which is to say that the idea survives outside the conversation. Therefore, externally, two conversations may proceed in entirely the same way, *social* in the inner sense, but only with all its value and charm can the essence find its justification, its place, its purpose, in the functional play of conversation and the form of the exchange of talk (*Redetausch*), which is special and particularly significant. Therefore, quick and easy changes of subject are part of the essence of social conversation, in which the subject is only a means to an end and comes with a complement of exchange and casualness. Overall, the means is in contrast to its own established goal.

As I said, sociability offers the only instance in which speech has a legitimate self-goal (*Selbstzweck*). Due to the fact that it is simply two-sided, and with the exception of the self-regarding (*Sich-Ansehens*) it is perhaps the most sublime two-sided form of all sociological manifestations. It is almost as fulfilling as a relationship, since the interaction (*Wechselwirkung*) is the essence of self-sufficiency. These combined interconnections also come from the telling of stories, jokes, and anecdotes and may often be fillers or an indication of lack of worth, but can also indicate a fine tact, which finds resonance in all of the motivations of sociability. Then, at the outset, the conversation is formed on a basis that stands beyond all individual intimacy, beyond the personal, and which will not be submitted to the categories of sociability. However, the objective is to advance the interests of sociability. That this is expressed and accepted is not a self-goal but the means for the vitality, the self-understanding, and the common consciousness of the circle. It is not only given a content in which all could equally participate; it is also the gift of the individual to the totality, but in such a way that the one behind the offering, so to speak, becomes invisible. The finest socially told story is the one that in the telling allows the teller to disappear into the background. That teller remains in the happy equilibrium of the so-called social ethic, in which the subjective individual, as well as the objective contents have fully dissolved in the service of the perfect form of sociability.

With this it is indicated that sociability is also the play form for the ethical forces of concrete society. The greatest of these forcefully presented problems is that the individual must live to integrate into a total relationship, but those values and enhancements flow back to him. That is, the life of the individual is a roundabout way for the whole to achieve its goals, but the life of the whole is also a roundabout path for the goals of the individual to travel. The seriousness or even tragic sense of these demands carries over into sociability and its symbolic play in its realm of shadows in which there is no friction, because shadows cannot hit one another. It may be a further ethical task of socialization to make finding oneself in the connection and in the separation of the elements from one's self to the more exact, sincere expression of the inner self through the determined relations of the totality of life. If so, within sociability, freedom and adequacy loosen their conditions from the concrete and the essential. And as 'social' groups build up and split, as the double conversation arises, drops down, solidifies, terminates according to its impulse and opportunity, they form a miniature picture of the ideal of sociability, what could be called freedom of bonding. While all 'with one another' and 'from one another' should be the strictly measured phenomena of inner realities, so have inner realities fallen away and only their appearance remains. That appearance remains in its own form and in the obeying play, in which the closed charm of that measurement which represents the *aesthetic* and the *ethical* demands of this decision form the seriousness of realities.

This complete significance of sociability has apparently come about from certain historical developments. In the early German Middle Ages, knightly brotherhoods were formed from friendly Patrician families. The religious and practical goals of this unity seem to have been lost early, and in the fourteenth century only the *knightly* interests and connections remained. Soon, even these disappeared and what remained was only the social unification of aristocratic strata. Thus, sociability obviously developed as the residue of a content-determined society – as the residue because the content had been lost, and only form and forms remain of the 'with one another' and 'for one another'. That the specific condition of these forms can be shown only in the inner essence of play or, fundamentally, of art emerges even more visibly in the court society (*Hofgesellschaft*) of the *ancien régime*. From the suppression of the essence of life that the French aristocracy brought about in certain ways through royalty and the development of free-floating forms, the consciousness of these classes crystallized. Forms, whose forces, determinations, and relationships were entirely social, are not symbols or functions of real significance and intensity of persons or institutions. The essence of etiquette, of court sociability, became a personal goal. It no longer signalled an essence, but etiquette gained validity only by being regarding as an art, with its own laws, so that anything outside that art did not have a purpose. And the reality of the model was truer and more real than a reproduction.

With this manifestation, sociability reached its most sovereign expression, but at the same time was transformed into an expression of caricature. Certainly, to cut the essence out of its central character – realistic interrelations (*Wechsel-bezeihungen*) – leaves the form set and without purpose outside its recognized relationships, having reached its heights. The deep source of sociability can be sought only in the attractive liveliness of the individual and in the fullness of his impulses and convictions. All sociability is only a *symbol* of life, as can be seen in the flow of light and happy play, yet it is still a symbol of *life*. It is also the freest and the most fantastic, since of all copies of reality the farthest removed art is still in a closer, deeper and truer relation to reality, as long as it is not defiled and seduced. If sociability cut the threads that bind it to the living reality, and through which it spins a stylized web, it becomes a game, a trifling with empty forms, something that is not alive.[11]

From this connection it is clear why humanity complains rightly and wrongly about the *superficiality* of human communication. This belongs to one of the most effective facts of spiritual existence, when, from the entirety of being we link together some elements into the spiritual realm, which follows its

11 Simmel's point is that sociability may be symbolic but that does not mean that it is artificial. Rather, Simmel insists that sociability needs to be bound up with life; and when it becomes divorced from life that it becomes artificial.

own laws and is not controlled by the whole. Obviously, this realm is entirely cut off from the life of the whole, with all inner completion, an empty nothing that can be shown as a floating essence in the air. It is often only through imponderables that it changes, and is distanced from all immediate reality, and it is the deepest essence of which can be shown as more complete, more unified, and more analogous than any attempt to grasp it more realistically and without the sense of distance. According to this or that perception that exists is the one and under one's own norms of the ongoing life, that the superficiality of social interactions (*Wechselwirkungen*) in sociability have been won and which have become formulaic, insignificant, lifeless – or a symbolic play, in which this aesthetic charm of all of the finest, sublime dynamic of social being in general and its realm is collected. We are dependent on the entire art, on the entire symbolism of religious and churchly life, and even in large part on the complex formulations of science, which are based on the faith (*Glaube*), on the feeling that the particular law-likeness of the parts of appearance, and [believe] that the combination of superficial elements possesses a relation to the deep totality of reality, that to each carrier and representative it is an immediately real and fundamental part of existence, even if this is often difficult to express.

From that we understand the saving and the happy effects of much of this – that from mere forms of existence a realm of riches has accumulated, within which we are saved from life, yet we still have it. As the view of the ocean frees us spiritually; not in spite of but rather, because of its roars, that it flows in order to ebb, and it ebbs in order to flow. Thus, the whole of life to the simplest expression of its dynamic seems entirely free from all lived reality and from all the difficulties of individual fate – and yet, appears to flow into the picture. In this sense, art reveals the secret of life: we do not release ourselves by simply looking away; but create and experience in the apparently vain play of its forms the sense and the power of its deepest reality, but without reality itself. For many people experience the depth and pressure of life every minute. And, society could not hold the freeing, releasing happiness, were it really only an escape from one's self, from this life, as if it were only a momentary lifting of its seriousness. Often enough, this is only a negative, a conventional and an internal, lifeless exchange of formulae – perhaps more so in the *ancien régime*, where the dull angst of a threatening reality pushed men into looking away from the powers of life. The release and uplifting that the inner human finds in sociability, in the togetherness and effective exchange that are drawn equally from all the tasks and all the weight of life, will be enjoyed here in the artistic play, in that simultaneous sublimating and thinning, in which the essential forces of reality and its difficulty evaporate, and from a distance seems only to be a suggestion of charm.

FERDINAND TÖNNIES

Ways and Goals of Sociology

[Thursday Morning 20 October 1910
Presiding: Professor Dr F. Tönnies (Kiel-Eutin)

Honoured assembled members!
I have the honour herewith in the name of the Presidium to open the First
German Sociological Conference.]

Were it permissible to speak, as is common practice today, in the very
comfortable style used in advertising, I would like to begin my speech with the
words: 'The future belongs to sociology'. However, I will be content with
expressing the expectation and hope that 'Sociology *has* a future'. However, I
have not discussed its present state – because that would be much too big a
theme – nor have I dealt with the matter of its possible future. But with your
permission, I will pursue the ways and goals of sociology that are appropriate
to the founding of our Society.

Sociology is first a philosophical discipline. As such, it is much older than its
name. The name did not create it, nor did the person who coined the name
bring it into being. Speculation about the essence of human society, especially
political alliances, has always been closely connected with the ideas of ethical
and good conduct of life and forms of life. Philosophers, who want to find the
right way and to lead, should be guides to life. The development of theoretical
sociology, which may also call be called 'social philosophy', is, then, inseparable
from the history of legal philosophy. Consequently, it is also inseparable from
the general doctrine of the state, from prosperity – in relation to which, in
recent times, theories have emerged about the best way to conduct economic
life; and these have branched off from their natural and legitimate connections,
that is, the relationship between production, exchange and consumption. At

57

the same time, we notice that all efforts at understanding these connections are slow and distance themselves only with difficulty from conscious motivations, in other words, from wishes, desires and practical ideas and tendencies. However, perhaps it is impossible to be fully and absolutely distanced from these conscious motivations. Everywhere in organic life there are oppositions: the normal and the abnormal; the physiological and the pathological; the healthy and the diseased; those who are living consciously and those who are declining. It is no wonder, then, that sociological thinking has always been intimately concerned with the natural, the normal, the right laws, with establishing the rational and the best state, and with ideal legislation brought about by nature or by reason. Accordingly, the doctrines of sociology appear to be a branch of general philosophical ethics, which it now perceives as its only concern – and has signified that it has won its independence and its individuality from the centre of philosophy.

To understand the connection between ethics and the fulfilment of wishes and desires is more than a coincidental necessity. It is, in fact, an essential connection, for all our thinking and knowing stand, fundamentally, at the service of wants. However crude the calling of utility may be, however little the application and utilization of his results may mean to the individual researcher, social appearances somehow *determine* the success and progress of all science. The binding threads that connect, carry and further social desires are thin, but social desires always arrange themselves around the struggle so as to overcome social evil insofar as is possible, and they wrestle around the form and the achievement of social good as the human ideal. It may remain to be determined whether there is absolute evil or absolute good for humanity. Philosophical ethics and legal philosophy in their traditional forms rest on the assumption that this question can be answered affirmatively. In the eighteenth century this was believed to be the case, but by the nineteenth century this view was regarded critically, even sceptically. However, even ethics and legal philosophy in their entirety, especially rational 'natural law', also have an objective, conceptual form of knowledge that is independent of the affirmation or denial of that question. Its sociological or socio-philosophical content even amounts to a doctrine of the possible, real (and necessary) *ethical* and *legal* connections, relations and associations of men. This doctrine can be extracted from 'natural law' in order to gain a piece of the most important theoretical sociology. The differentiation, separation and division of labour all contribute to the great law of development. Therefore, the sciences grow and expand, in order to be stronger and to separate and free themselves more from the immediate and resultant influences of the tendencies of the will towards practical interests. Indeed, the more they go their own way and elevate the knowledge of concepts and their interconnections and consequents, and of facts, their causes and their effects, on personal human goals, the more they leave to scientists decisions about whether to make use of the results of thinking and research. This leitmotiv has not yet found sufficient recognition and appreciation in regard to the concepts and facts of social life. The idea of wholly theoretical insight, of the study and observation of the social operations of our environment as if they were operations of a moon and mean nothing to us, and the idea of the study and observation of human passions and strivings as if they were the angles of a triangle or calculable curves is still seen as being foreign to the public service aspects of our discipline. Obviously, in German universities the theoretical economy has been separated from the practical political economy. This signifies, however, a great step forward for theory, and it is also valid for the political economy as practised by the people (*Volkswirtschaftspolitik*), and for studying state legislation that regulates and has affected economic life in the past and continues to do so. Political economy is mainly historical and statistical in nature and the science cares nothing for an enquiry into what should be and what is wholesome and *correct*. Few scholars, when freely and honourably convinced that a certain policy is correct, would discard their concern for the common good in favour of other reasons and interests, and would not reject every suspicion of non-scientific motivation. Their intention is to be like the physician at the patient's bedside, who decides on the basis of a well-thought out, accurate *diagnosis*, to prescribe a remedy that works to heal the sick person or at least retard the illness; or like the dietician, who orders a dietary regime to conserve health and strengthen the body.

In fact, even the public knows enough to give proper attention to the differences between a valid argument for free trade made by a famous scholar and the same view expressed by the owner of a firm with interests in global trade. It is not expected that the opinion of the company owner should be determined by anything other than his own interests, while an impartial judgement is expected of the scholar, who should stand above interested parties and their interests. This can be the response in no small measure, if at the same time it is not excluded that his judgements, his estimations of values, his striving and his entire personality, with his character, his temperament, his *Weltanschauung* or world view, are essentially determined through his lineage and education. In the same way, his feelings, inclinations and disinclinations are also, through his personal and subjective connections, rooted to his surroundings and his past. Moreover, it is not possible to be fully free from the influences, or, should we say, from the bonds of wants and wishes. Even someone who wants to base the entirely subjective on a universal, on the objective-factual, even to be inextricably tied up with it, part of that person withdraws from it, usually for *one* reason, such as feeling or mood. Only from this it is possible to see that every interested and political *party* has its thinker, its spiritual and scientific promoter, its perhaps objective impartial colleagues or party comrades who, unlike the adviser, secretary and speaker, will not be paid in money, but at most in respect (*Achtung*) and honour – for we may accept 'that they are all, all honour values' and honour them.

Physicians consulting even at the sick-bed also have differing opinions, not only regarding the diagnosis of the illness, its foreseeable course, etc. but also about the proper treatment with the most appropriate drugs (*zweckmäßigen Heilmittel*).[1] At least here the goal is clearly and easily understandable: the health and the longest possible life of the patient. Certainly, we also all want the health and the longest possible life for our people (*Volk*) or, obviously from an entirely different standpoint: humanity; West European culture; or however else we may like to describe our ideal – even when we hold fast to our nation. It is not so easy to recognize the signs of health or sickness in a simple sensible essence (*Wesen*) [that is, Germany] as it is in a human individual. The analogy fails in many places in the same way when applied to social bodies or organisms. Medicine is also a conjectural and error-laden art, but we trust in ourselves, we trust our most precious body to the expert opinion of a physician, and in difficult cases to the decisions of a committee, and obviously we reserve for ourselves or for the sick the decision on whether a life-threatening operation should be carried out. In *social pathology*, the patient and the doctor are not at the same time sharply and clearly separate people. The nation can speak only through representatives, who may be called or chosen, and these want at the same time to be their doctors. If some of these representatives are judged to be sick, there is in no way a dominant agreement regarding that; not to mention any agreement regarding the nature of the illness or the location of the malady. If, in some given cases there is an agreement of the legislative factors from which a voting majority is reached, and that is compared with the results of physicians' treatment, it is almost always highly questionable whether and how far these factors are only a *claim* based on a correct *scientific* judgement. Factually, there are scientifically unfounded wishes and wants that are regular and are recognized as being the deciding factor. This is so when the mood and more or less limited understanding of a man is the same as that of groups of wild people who are led to find wisdom by the inspiration of a shaman

---

1 Discussions of methods and goals are often associated with Weber, but Tönnies deals with the topic here, as well as in his contribution to the two-volume work in honour of Weber's death. See Ferdinand Tönnies, 'Zweck und Mittel im sozialen Leben', in *Hauptprobleme der Soziologie. Erinnerungsausgabe für Max Weber*. Ed. Melchior Palyi. München und Leipzig: Verlag von Duncker & Humblot, 1923. 235–70.

(*Zauberpriester*, literally, 'magic priest') and by the grace of the *gods*, if the recognition of this type of power is present in the state as well as in the church.

Whether superstition is essentially an element of the *power* and *strength* of will and energy, whether lack of energy is associated with superstitious thoughts, remains to be considered separately. I maintain that it is in the highest degree, and it is equally an element of all passions and inspirations, and of all prejudices and preconceived opinions held by members of political parties, and of the blindness and simplicity of spirit that often in innocents 'gets', what no understanding of the one who sees, 'gets'. But, it is also [too] confident—where reflection makes one sceptical and cautious. Yet recognition of the element of superstition will never move us to trust in a childlike spirit in any sense in our destiny: *we are reasonable, enlightened, mature men*, so the building of our houses or ships depends as little on natural or supernatural inspirations as does legislation to fight social maladies, or even the healing of our bodies. *Whether* we are reasonable, enlightened and mature, and how many of us are presently involved in the well-being of the community (*Gemeinwohles*) is another question.

Even in its dark moods, humanity is still sufficiently well aware of the right ways, of the fact that reason and science represent its highest powers and that they will always rely on them, and that the more powerful they are, the more they *will be* internalized, so that they will be trusted.

We must not allow ourselves to be confused over the fact that scientific knowledge must be the factor that determines the validity of even *political* practice, that through scientific knowledge the wishes of party members can be elevated to the wishes of the people, and that the knowledge of the statesman of what is the correct, healing action at least approximates to the physician's security and certainty about what to do. With this knowledge, the statesman will understand how to fulfil his duty in dealing with legislative bodies.

May sociology place itself in the light of these great thoughts of the future, just as the creator of its name considered the same point of view. For him, however, 'positive politics' signified a strictly scientific positivism, by contrast with theological and metaphysical prejudices and suppositions.

None of us believes that the matter is as simple as August Comte believed it to be. He meant to establish it sufficiently through his *philosophy of history* and through his law of the three stages of recognition of the programme for our age, according to a schema that is entirely the analogue to the Hegelian dialectic of Thesis-Antithesis-Thesis.[2] To sum up: the task of scientific politics is to

2 The French thinker Auguste Comte divided history into three periods: the theological; the metaphysical; and the positivist. Positivism, with its emphasis on science and mathematics, replaces the prejudices and the ideology found in the first two.

revolutionize the social order that began in the Middle Ages as theological politics within the church, which bound freedom and progress, and in its negation is called metaphysical politics, in order to recreate it.

We leave all programmes of the future, all social and political tasks, out of play, not because we despise them, but as a consequence of scientific thought, because we note the difficulties of basing such ideas scientifically and for the time being consider them unconquerable; and because we are separated from those who have other intentions, e.g. 'scientific socialism', we expect that there will be an agreement that we will cast such controversial matters (*Streitfragen*, literally 'strife questions') from the domain of sociology, and will limit ourselves to the more easily resolvable task of the *objective knowledge of facts* (*objektiver Erkenntnis der Tatsachen*). When, eventually, we must also concede that complete objectivity signifies an unattainable ideal, we can *strive* with all the energy of the will to attain knowledge, and through such striving bring ourselves *closer* to it, but to an indeterminable degree. That is our programme.

As sociologists, we want to be concerned only with what *is*, not with what some specified intention based on some specified grounds *should be*. Our next objective is the present reality of social life in its immeasurable diversity. A glance necessarily extends from it into the past, back to the beginning and the germination of the existing, to the fall of institutions and the world of ideas, and we also glance into the future, not to form or to direct it, but merely as a *prognosis*, to predict the likely development of existing conditions, orders and perceptions, and the foreseeable after-effects such knowledge would have on the activities of man. Foreknowledge can be a contributory factor in our activities, can be introduced into the calculations and can modify the prognosis.

I began from the principle that sociology is first a philosophical doctrine. As such, it is essentially involved with concepts – with the concepts of social life, social relations, social forms of will (*Willensformen*), social values and social ties. Among other concepts are the concepts of custom (*Sitte*), and of law, religion and public opinion, church and state. Sociology must develop these concepts, that is, it must make them suitable for use, it must forge and chisel them in order that the facts of experience can be used to hang things on, as if on a nail, or to fasten on to things, like a clamp. In this area, sociology has not so much to do with the knowledge of facts directly, but is concerned with producing the most useful, the most suitable tool for such knowledge. This is an exceedingly important task, which the empiricist minimizes, often to his detriment. An example of this short-sighted under-estimation occurred in 1841, when the editor of a then-respected physics journal received Julius Robert Mayer's work 'On the Quantitative and Qualitative Determination of Powers', which contained the entire cell nucleus of modern energetics. The editor not only deemed it unworthy to give a single reply; he even neglected to send the manuscript back, as had been requested. Examples of equivalent short-sightedness are also found in the annals of the social sciences.

However, philosophical sociology has another task, beyond this *sculpture of concepts.* It wants to trace the connections between the social and other sciences, in the sense defined earlier by Comte and Spencer. For philosophy wants the unity of knowledge, it wants to derive as much as possible from simple principles, and it wants to *deduce* from the necessary principles of being and thinking. The universal laws of appearances, material as well as spiritual, material and spirit, spirit as material, are conditioned and determined by the laws of thinking (*Denkgesetze*). They also necessarily support the facts of life, that is, human social life. The conservation of energy must penetrate appearances in an economy, as it must in law and in politics, and permeate cultural phenomena in the entire world of thought, and may be further recognizable as limitless entanglements and as dependencies. These entanglements provoke speculative thinking, as when we admire this behaviour in much the same way that we enjoy the giddiness that comes from climbing enticing mountain paths, even when they lead the wrong way, and when accidents follow. A great example of this monistic Alp-thinking (*Gedanken-Alpinismus*) has also been provided by Herbert Spencer in the application of sociology, when in the most genial manner he attempted to develop formulae for *development* from the universal principles of movement. His success was limited, but the greatness of his will can be emulated only by one who can succeed in a similar work with fewer defects. However justifiable criticisms of Spencer may be, he was a powerful, serious and great thinker, of whom we will not see the likes again.

The deductive procedure of sociology must especially be based on the truths of *biology* and *psychology*, for social life is an appearance of *life* and the being of the individual, whose existence is not necessarily presupposed. Here lie the origins, but also here lie the limited sense of the 'biological analogies' and the organizational aspects of social life. But, psychology fosters the demands for their necessary completion, so that what can be thought are now instincts, complacencies, superstitions, or those known desires and conscious interests that are the binding elements between men. The simplest social relations can also be observed among animals, so that some vague notion could be maintained of the existence of a so-called 'animal state' from primeval times. The laws of life are also wholly universal, for the facts of human life – the constant changing of matter and the perpetual reproduction, the laws of conservation and propagation are what the *population* regards as carriers of a social system. Even so, we can abstract from the universal causes of animalistic desires and their feeling of the apparent, indeed, of more or less certain effects on every human community and society. In the expanding culture they are infinitely manifest: but their characteristic features are easily recognized again in all economic, political and spiritual cultures.

These types of culture condition and penetrate one another. They establish the natural separation between sexes and between generations, the difference between the rulers and the ruled, between estates and classes, the contrast between city and country, wars and competition between neighbours, the commonality and the *division of labour*, the expansion of exchange and of trade. They are found in all the power of transference, delivery, of origin, in customs (*Sitten*) and – it follows – in justice, and so in courts and in law. These, in the closest interconnection with the last-named powers [i.e. custom, justice, and the courts], the influence of superstitious representations, and religion, are therefore valid in earthly essence and have their earthly representatives in priests. It is in developments in the expanding but also in the reformed power of increasing experience and especially of those in capitalism, in the state and science, that the growing, generalizing *thinking* has brought about a 'revolution' – although that is something that was not unknown in earlier civilizations. And the developments have been justified through their astonishing effects on technology, and on judicial and spiritual life during the last four centuries, especially during the nineteenth and into the beginning of the twentieth century.

Here, we find ourselves enmeshed in a network of difficult problems, which the exciting questions devour, and which are batted back and forth in the conflicts of modern political parties. The sociologist, as we understand him, does not volunteer to solve any of these problems. Instead, he imposes strict abstinence upon himself and does not do those things that a person in the role of politician would do. However, the sociologist must still strive to unravel these problems, to learn conceptually and genetically to understand them, and thus perhaps to contribute to a more sensible, even to a passionless, conception of these world-shaking questions. What is valid for social questions in general is valid even more so for closely related concerns and reforms: as sociologists, we are neither for nor against socialism, neither for or against the expansion of women's rights, neither for nor against the mixing of races; however, we find in all of these questions, in socio-political as in socio-educational and social hygiene problems, and for knowledge based on facts. To these questions sociology finds its limits, without usurping related ideas and struggles, without wanting to advance or to hinder something else. Whether advancement or hindrance springs out of the right knowledge is another question. In general, it can certainly be expected.

However, this entire domain is not the private domain of a sociological society. Philosophy of history and social life will always carry with them the expression of the unifying conception of *individual* spirits that the learning, co-operating, continuing, enhancing and capable disciples should be; but a school is something other than an association. A scientific society rests upon the *equality* of its active, regular members; even its wider membership regards itself more as a supporting than a receiving body. In the narrower sense it exists through citizens who contribute to the common goals, in our case from specialists of many different disciplines, some of whom are involved in the social sciences, and have therefore at least partly expressed that aspect of themselves.

We are not dealing here with a system, nor with a few more or less established theories, nor with concepts or deductions, but with research and investigation. The method is observation and induction. The task is to collect scientific experiences of many different ways of life and give them a sociological focus. Certainly, conceptual explanations, along with problems of pure sociology can be explained inside an association, and we really wish that it may happen. However, the working together, the co-operation in following a plan is an alternative to debate. It is a necessary factor in the forging of a powerful organization.

All such research can win power and grow through the orientation of conceptual and systematic sociology, inasmuch as the concepts are purposeful, the deductions are exact. It is therefore imperative that sociology be based on empirical research, on confirmation and correction, that its concepts are always revised and its deductions tested and verified, so that it will always recognize the truth, and that every source of factual knowledge is critically examined – trustworthy conclusions cannot be derived from a single or several connected causes, since reality is too complicated and too many influences underlie it. Rules need to be used to arrive at adequate explanations. To be able to grasp the rational as well as the empirical, deductive and inductive thinking must be used to explain highly significant problems, for example, the relations between economic, political and spiritual expressions of interconnected human lives and to lead to a solution. Only by this method can, for example, a discussion of the so-called materialist understanding of history – Marxism – be fruitful.

Sociology based on empirical research can, however, only be put together from multiple results derived from methodical and inductive research. Its contributions will be dedicated, received and retained by each of the sciences, which will be enriched as a result of the reciprocity between the related branches of knowledge.

I will consider first those sciences that have a connection with social life. By its nature, *anthropology* stands foremost. Its logical concepts grasp the totality of the social life of humans as object; its real concepts must, however, be limited to the consideration of individual humans from specific points of view.

Sociological Beginnings

Anthropology is understood differently and limited in different ways in different countries. Consider its teaching in the German-speaking realm, where man is presented as having physical, spiritual and social sides. Under each of these points, humanity is separated into races and sub-races, into natural peoples and tribes, as a foundation for the observation of the various hereditary predispositions and inclinations, to provide a scientific insight into the development of humanity and the destiny of peoples. The question of the relative portion of this and of the usual natural factors that can be clustered together according to their complementarity as being the background for research into a culture is one of the most significant tasks of sociological analysis. This must be supported by anthropological and by other natural scientific research, including geological and, especially, geographical research. In this sense 'Anthro-geography' is a special area of work (*Arbeitsgebiet*) and which is tied to others. Geography and anthropology cannot, in fact, be separated from each another; therefore, even the sociological view also must always be drawn back to the geographical facts.

Psychology, as it is generally understood as the doctrine of the psychic life of individual humans, would fall entirely within the purview of anthropology in a logical classification of the sciences. However, it may be interpreted as a doctrine of psychic life *in general*, so that it does not have sufficient reason to focus on *individual* humans and is then faced with the facts of general – collective – psychic life, from which the individual must be largely derived and explained. This observation has been scientifically developed under a compound name: the term 'folk-psychology' (*Völkerpsychologie*) was coined in Germany and more currently is propagated through the work of one master. *Wundt* once compared the three areas of common spiritual life that he initially wanted to present with his 'folk-psychology' with the trinity of representation (presentation: *Vorstellung*), feeling and will in individual consciousness.[3] The sociological and psychological views of the confirmations of the folk-spirit (*Volksgeist*) lie close to each another. The differences lie in their connections with ethnic psychic life, which occur in different forms. These may be evident as the essence of a people or a tribe as reflected in speech, belief in gods, their temples or churches and their religious cults and priests, and the essence of duties and rights that are reflected in their social relations and associations, prescribed by custom (*Sitte*) and offered respect (*Achtung*). Moreover, social cohesion expresses itself in relationships and in the varied understanding and

---

3 Wilhelm Wundt (1832–1920) stressed experimentalism and can be credited with making psychology into a credible science. He also believed that there was something to the notion of a 'spirit' of a certain group of people, hence his conviction that the study of *Völkerpsychologie* was important.

in the consciousness of the simplest expressions of the forms of social will and social thinking; that is, in customs (*Sitte*) and religion. As such, they are the first objects of *social psychology* – which, however, through these observations is transformed into sociology and must reveal itself in the formation and development of concepts. *Folk-psychology*, as its name indicates, combines mainly psychology and folk-ethnology – a branch of knowledge that has separated, ethnography being the description of customs and usages (*Sitten und Gebräuche*) and economic, political and spiritual institutions, and the religions and *Weltanschauungen* (world views) of the observed peoples (*Völkerschaften*). As ethnology is the doctrine of the peoples of the Earth, including these social facts, it is dedicated to the sociological task. On the basis of knowledge of contemporary social conditions of an uncultivated people, it seeks to uncover the *development of culture*, under the supposition that the primitive and embryonic forms of institutions and ideas meet in so-called 'natural peoples', and that they *represent* the initial stages of the development of cultured peoples, so that even when a people under study are not the same as a cultured people, they are still very similar, permitting analogies to be constructed. Remains and traces have supported the view that there is a general similarity between older and newer phases of development. As this *comparison* in general is the great principle of scientific knowledge, it was the first proper validation in the natural sciences in the nineteenth century. Comparisons of peoples and groups of people and their witnesses have generated many studies. While previously they were undertaken on a speculative basis, they are now given a positive basis, in particular, studies relevant to the universal science of language, the universal doctrine of law and the study of religions. For empirical sociology, the *comparison* of social life is incontestable, and at the least, very significant preparations have been made. I will have occasion to come back to this.

I linger on related subjects for research, and must above all think of the *historical* disciplines, which draw on the entire domain of human social life. Sociology necessarily has a particularly strong relationship to them – if a difficult one. Two thinkers – one who invented the name 'sociology' and another who has been most effective in spreading it around the globe – both believed sociology to be almost exclusively the philosophical study of history. Spencer believed that it indicated concrete knowledge of the development of humanity; and Comte saw it as the positive-scientific doctrine of state and society as they *should* be. I do not want to judge the value of these views, which may rapidly become antiquated, so as not to demolish the sense of the *task*. The *idea* of a philosophical study, which may want above all to concentrate on the *logic* of history and the writing of history, cannot be rejected. In addition, universal history is the necessary task of the *history-writer* and of the scientific history-

67

writer, whose essence is like that of an artist when he dips his pen into the ink, which is mixed from biological, psychological, and sociological ingredients. For its problem is the development of social beings: one biological – the development of culture; and one socio-psychological – the development of peoples, societies, churches and states – a sociological problem, even if they merge into others and have a share in others. Thus, if the universal historian is to a certain degree a sociologist, it does not follow that the sociologist must somehow be a universal historian. He will leave history to the historian as ethnology is left to the ethnologist. Historic, prehistoric, ethnological and anthropological researches and results are of great importance to him, in that all have a sociological aspect. However, the sociologist cannot want to concur with specialists or interpreters still less so with the researchers in these fields, even though a personal union with a particular one is always possible. A historical view and knowledge of the object of research is undeniably important for empirical sociology, history is not the object of sociological study and investigation. Empirical sociology must grow on the basis of real social sciences, which offer the possibility of an ideal *unity*, through which its point of view will be illuminated. Lately, and still always defectively incomplete, there are two separations in the social sciences: 1) which has already been discussed, is the doctrine of the separation of that which in some sense should be from research into that which is; and 2), the separation of conceptual exposition and deduction from research into facts through observation to complete and useful application.

By this it is easy to recognize that the doctrine of that which should be is closely connected with conceptual exposition and deduction, but does not cover them. Even so, research into what is has induction as its main source, thus it rests on the research of the facts. Accordingly, it will not collapse together again, so that two new separations and delineations are made necessary.

The development of differentiations and separations has been most prominent in *political economy* and has burdened that careful social science with conflicts over opinions, without it having yet yielded a complete clarification. Theoretical national economy is inseparable from theoretical or pure sociology; it is, in fact, part of it and the part that is now ripe for sociological treatment and discussion. The doctrine of the people's economy (*Volkswirtschaftslehre*) belongs to empirical sociology, but as it is an integrated part of it, is observed, analysed, reported and investigated as real economic *life*. This research can, however, at no point be completed without first being extended to other aspects of social life. Like other partial research in this area, it is referred to and drawn out from the totality of social states and movements – which is a significant characteristic of sociological as opposed to historical science: history runs from the past, sociology runs from the present. The past and the present merge into each other, and are connected by 1,000 threads and are members of one and the same development. Obviously, therefore, the historian must always, to a certain degree, be a sociologist and the sociologist must always be in part a historian. The historian will still first relate and report how the past was and perhaps touch on how the present has come to be. The sociologist will first describe the present as it is, as its many aspects determine and support one another, but also wrestle and fight with each other. The sociologist will also discuss how they appear in the reciprocal events of the present expansion and hindering of the picture of culture, and how it retains its expression through human willingness and ability. The historian can, in addition, be concerned with the *legality* of past changes, and will want to describe them, to go back over them. He can employ comparative methods to set out the similarities and differences in the development of institutions and social forms among different groups of people, among the same people in different areas, and among different tribes. However, his *next* scientific activity will always be tied to the development of the factual, with how it was in the past. Today is no longer open to observation, so the farther his object of study is from present interests and passions, the more certain will he feel in his historical objectivity, and the more secure will he be in falling back on his *value judgements* (*Werturteile*). The reason is that from a distance, through the establishment of further temporal effects, the historian has clear knowledge of the development of a people or even of the whole of humanity as it has thrived or in its destruction. The sociologist sets against this his objectivity 1) refraining from value judgements; and 2) the application of measurements and numbers to describe and to compare facts.

It may be regarded as coincidental, but it is at least an ingenious coincidence, that from the *statistics* of the eighteenth century, which were used mainly in the founding of states and which have been described as 'curiosities' like coats of arms and other signs of distinction of what once was, today has emerged as statistics. That is, it is a representation of circumstances and proceedings in *numbers*, and relationships between those numbers and other numbers – a methodological principle that is implicit in induction. Clearly, in spite of and within this related significance of the concept, *statistics as science* is established and extended. In modern times, statistics have received the most approval through the authority of its Italian and German representative as the *application* in a narrower or material sense – but, it is statistics in the wider or formal sense that it should be understood regarding the state and the society of living human beings.

Mr Georg von Mayr has defined statistics more exactly as the universal science of social masses, and still more precisely as an explanation based on observation of a state from the perspective of the numbers and measurements relating to that state and the manifestations of human social life, inasmuch as it is possible to express human social life in numbers.[4]

Clearly, these conceptual determinations (*Begriffsbestimmungen*) have sprung from linguistic adaptations of the *word* 'statistics'.[5] I do not believe it permissible to take a quantitative determination with the concept of an object of a science. Even less so can the essence of a science be created by the *application of a method*. If it were possible at this moment, despite difficulties, to rip away the concept of statistics as a science from the word 'statistics', as appears to have happened, as Wundt has suggested in his doctrine of methodology (*Methodenlehre*) that the concept of statistics as a science or in other words then we could fully give the name of statistics to a specific science. Statistics is known first and foremost as the states and changes of a given *population* that can be expressed as an empirical object. 'Population is the statistical element par excellence.'[6] The statistical presentation and investigation of *economic* facts: production and consumption, trade and commerce, worker conditions, the national economy inasmuch as it will be a science of facts, will not be taken away. They belong to it and must serve it, if at the same time they are relevant to the discipline, and especially when taken over by official statistics. All conditions and movements of social life will be divided into the most appropriate economic, political and spiritual [spheres]. Mass observation is as valid as the characteristics of statistical science (it is really a characteristic of statistical method), and will stretch themselves over all three genre. The bare numbers of people (*Volksmenge*), the number of inhabitants of a country or a community, a region, etc, even when important for economic science, are essentially *political* facts. Their presentation and investigation according to numbers and relations between numbers is 'political arithmetic' in the old sense of the term. Clearly, these figures stand in close contact with *natural* facts and can be understood as the biological side of social life and are directly indicated by *economic* life. This is valid for much of the numerical information that falls into the categories of medical statistics, criminal statistics, or more generally as moral statistics. These belong overwhelmingly with the

---

4 I have found little in reference to Mayr, but Tönnies probably has in mind his *Die Gesetzmäßigkeit in Gesellschaftsleben*, 1877. Mayr's interest in statistics is found later in his life in his *Moralstatistik*, 1917.

5 The following paragraphs are rather unclear. Tönnies' points seem to be that for statistics to be taken seriously as a science it needs to move away from its linguistic origins and recognize that it encompasses more than mere numbers. It is also political, economic, and 'spiritual'.

6 'La population est l'élement statistique par excellence.' Tönnies does not attribute this saying to anyone.

objects of educational statistics, etc., to the *spiritual* facts of social life, which we always also count as *moral.*

We need a universal terminus for such a natural scientific study of men in their social states and fluxes, in particular in the law-abidingness of its arbitrary (*willkürlichen*)[7] activities, that with us we have only an inessential form of man, that the 'middle', the universal average man remains. It is as correct to think of this concept as principle-scientifically as it is as abstracting from its manifold appearances. But, it is still more important from all sides to be acquainted with (and can anticipate) men who are conditioned and determined through our economic, political, and spiritual relations. The happily found expressions *demography* and *demology* present themselves freely through the origin and use that it has a closer relation partially to the statistical method and partially to the facts of the population. But, both relations are not relevant to the expressions and have nothing to do with its etymology. Instead, they are fittingly suited, so that the cultural people (*Kulturvölker*) in its essence, in its economic-political constitution, in its spiritual life's manifestations, are drawn up as an object of the inductive and comparative scientific knowledge, so that its contents are fully united with the ethnography and ethnology. In fact, the most important works of the reported population statistics of today are of the type that the statistical method alone does not serve.[8] As Mr von Mayr said, that this cannot be thought (I would say: fully not the social facts as such) — that it is submitted to the exhaustive mass observations for there always remains certain aspects of conditions and operations. Numbers and measurements are not solely applicable to objective and exhaustive methods of observation, which is most successful with qualitative research carried out through collective and individual observations. As for the population – the land and the people – new methods of study must be found, which may or may not include the statistical method, but which allows expansion of knowledge by new means about the facts of vocations and jobs, property, power and justice, from the regularity and extraordinary occurrences of life to the movements of population. The high value of the statistical method does not rest solely on qualitative determinations. They are expanded and secured quantitatively – which is the true soul of scientific thinking in general – and that makes it possible to differentiate more exactly fixed relationships from other types: the relations are gradated according

7 *Willkür* and its derivatives are notoriously difficult to translate. For Tönnies, something is *willkürlich* if it is 'arbitrary' or simply 'chosen'. In *Gemeinschaft und Gesellschaft* he connects a variation (*Kürwille*) which is ideal and constructed whereas its opposite (*Wesenwille*) is real and natural. See Tönnies, 1979: 73–76.

8 Again Tönnies acknowledges the importance of statistics but he also insists that numbers do not and cannot tell the whole story. Qualitative methods and analyses are equally if not more important, especially in areas that do not lend themselves to quantitative study.

to the degree of fixity, so that it is possible to determine an exact comparison between the differences of appearances in space and time. This does not depend on the greater number, but the greater the number of observations, the more clearly are the opposing tendencies revealed and contrasted as well as in the raising, continuing, essential, necessary, thus, in the causal relations. In order to posit the real, we must also deal with the necessary, and posit the certain, which often come through the probable. We must use the most exact determination of probability, but – and here is one of the most significant points of social science, although it is taken mainly from its biological elements – we must reconnect to the mathematical-logical deduction.

Whether we cultivate statistics or whether we content ourselves with other forms of investigation, with 'extra-statistical orientation', as von Mayr termed it, to enhance our perspectives, we must always concern ourselves with true facts relating to how we want to expand, based on the most complete description possible. We in this Society seriously want to work assiduously to raise the study of social life above all political strife, to free it from the paralyzing weight of value judgements – to provide it as closely as possible with the certainty of mathematics and the accuracy of astronomy. The word 'sociology' has become, despite hostility, a global word (*Weltword*, literally 'world word') and, therefore, a carrier of thoughts worldwide (*Welt-Gedankens*, literally 'world thoughts'). The hostility is usually directed towards the name, which like other names is an invention of convenience. In addition to this useful function, it has the superiority of being an international word. Linguistically it is no worse than other scientific names, 'planimetry', for example. Even the universally accepted word 'biology' is linguistically falsely constructed; for life in the biological sense means ζώη in Greek.[9] Since it was founded, the word 'biology' has slowly become pervasive, and also the word 'sociology'. We strive to become pervasive with it, although this is obviously an infinite task.

Honoured ladies and gentlemen! Goethe took an expression from the English poet, Pope: 'The proper study of mankind is man'.[10] In the imperative form, this expression carries with it the old commandment from the Delphic God that so deeply moved Socrates, the commandment Γνώθι σεαυτον ('know thyself!'). Obviously, in the first instance that is a commandment directed at the individual, ethical man. It is an attempt, based on the dominance of reason, to accomplish this in him. Self-knowledge is the preparation for self-mastery. The commandment is also valid for *humanity*, for scientific man who, in the name of humanity, is called upon to think and to

9 Tönnies' point here is the Greek distinction between 'life' ζώη as a biological term versus the term 'life' Βίος as in a biography.
10 Tönnies uses the English here.

speak about being and becoming. Sociology is the impartial attempt to do justice to this commandment. Through it and in it will humanity know itself and there is the implicit hope that through self-knowledge, humanity will learn to master itself. This hope is embedded in the strict theoretical position we take. Everyone is free to create hope in his own way. Neither as man, nor as citizen of the state, nor as world citizen, nor as contemporary citizen (*Zeitbürger*), can anyone be indifferent to this hope. As thinkers and researchers, however, we are indifferent towards all the results and consequences of our thoughts and investigations. Just as there is only *one* sun for our planetary system, however many potential suns there may be in the universe, there is only *one* sun for a scientific system: the truth.

[Honoured guests,
The foundation of this Society was tied to scientific plans, with wishes and ideas more or less expressed of greater co-operation in the domain of research – and this reveals itself in agreement with my discussion, as is evidenced by the social life that surrounds us here.

First and foremost we are dealing with an enormous task: the public is counting on us to educate ourselves and them on the basis of lively interest and research.

I give the floor to Professor Max Weber to deliver his report on this.]

MAX WEBER

Business Report
followed by
The Comparative Sociology of
Newspapers and Associations

[Thursday Morning, 20 October 1910
Professor Dr Max Weber (Heidelberg)]

Ladies and Gentlemen
The business report of our Society, which I have the obligation to present, essentially ranges over:

1. The constitutional changes which the Society has initiated in the course of the past year; and
2. The concrete scientific tasks that the society has set itself for the near future.

The essence of the concept of 'sociology' being unstable, it is well for a society (*Gesellschaft*) with such an unpopular name to define what it wants to be through the wholly concrete specifications of the current constitution; and through the tasks it currently anticipates taking on.

On the first point, the following principles – which I will note briefly – were first expressed in our statutes during the course of last year. First: a principle my esteemed colleague, the previous speaker, has already discussed – that the Society fundamentally and definitively rejects any propaganda of *practical* ideas that might spring from its midst. The Society is not somehow only 'non-partisan' in the sense that it should be just, that it should understand all, or that it should want to seek to draw that beloved 'middle line' between party opinions, between political, socio-political, ethical or aesthetic values, or values of other types. Instead, it should have absolutely nothing to do with such opinions, so that in all areas it is simply party-*less* (*Partien-los*).[1] Thus, it is possible to make a purely objective investigative *analysis*, in which the existence, the individuality,

1 Weber emphasizes the Society's independence from all party viewpoints.

74

the demands and the successes of political, aesthetic, literary, religious and other party opinions can be discussed; and even the object of the analysis can be discussed as a *fact of its existence*; and the Society can judge the presumed or real reasons for the opinions, and their success or chances of success, and focus on their 'principle' and their 'practical' consequences. But never, as is stated in our current Statute §1, can the pros and cons, the value or lack of value, of any such opinion be the object of discussion in our Society. If, for example, the Society arranged an investigation (*Enquete*) into journalism (*Zeitungswesen*) – I will speak on that subject – so, according to our principles on such investigations, it would not be remotely possible to sit in judgement on facts about any current situation concerning journalism revealed during the investigation and the Society will not question the desirability or otherwise of such a situation. We must have no involvement with the subject of journalism other than to determine what it is; why it is as it is; and the historical and social reasons for its existence.

The second principle we have established is that the Society promotes no academic interests (*Akademismus*, literally, 'academic sense'). It is not a certifying body (*Notabilitätsgesellschaft*); it is exactly the opposite of anything like an academy. For example, no-one should be insulted who does not happen to have been invited to join one of the Society's committees, for it should not be an 'honour' (although it sounds rather paradoxical) to belong to this committee. This is because committee membership amounts merely to a statement that involvement in the tasks of the Society is temporarily structured in such a way that those gentlemen who have joined a committee have done so partly because they made their inclinations known to us on their own initiative; and partly because we asked them to join us as co-workers for the purpose of completing *this* particular task; and that they fulfil a single, universal precondition: namely, that for exclusively scientific – and therefore not practical – reasons, and on a basis that is free from any party strife, they will work with us on exclusively sociological tasks. The Society is task-oriented (*Arbeitsgemeinschaft* – literally, a 'work society'), but not, I repeat, equivalent to some 'academy'. Anyone who wants to join us on our terms is warmly welcomed.

Third, we have established the principle that the Society promotes no partisan interests,[2] that it sees itself as being the goal, that it does not seek to appropriate tasks for itself by drawing them away from others; in other words, that it wholeheartedly supports the principle of decentralization of scientific work.

That principle is expressed in our Constitution, first in the point that the

---

2 Weber uses the term *Ressort-patriotismus*, literally, 'department patriotism'.

work of the Society does not lie exclusively in meetings of the members, but in tasks delegated to committees appointed by the Society. The Society selects these committees so that the Chairmen and possibly a few members – the smallest possible number – have full sovereignty over their committee, particularly in co-opting other members of the Society and, indeed non-members where appropriate. This is particularly true of professionals – for example, in the area of journalism, a newspaper publisher and representative journalists, without whom we could not work, belong on our committees. As committee members they have full voting rights just as we do, and they have equal status in every respect; and we all work together, so that we will – we hope – benefit from direct stimulation from them.

The second issue that is expressed as part of the same principle of decentralization is that the sociological Society will never again do what it is doing today, that is, deal with a whole series of single themes one after another in speeches and in discussions. We propose to overcome this tendency by allowing the formation of various sub-groups. A sub-group on statistics has already been formed by a circle of statisticians. The Society has adopted the principle that it will not force the formation of sub-groups – the reverse, in fact. Interested parties in the relevant fields are entrusted to form groups of experts (*Fach-Abteilungen*, literally, 'expert sections'). The Board will then negotiate with these sub-groups over their position in the Society, and it is expected that they will be made as independent as possible. For their part, they are entrusted with ensuring that specialists and *only* specialists will be included in their group and they will exclude anyone whom they do not believe to be experts or specialists. The members of these sub-groups are to decide for themselves which tasks they want to take up and how they approach them.

For future sociological meetings, then – let us say in two years, or in a year and a half – assuming that sub-groups will be formed by other interested people – there can be simultaneous sessions; with, perhaps, a sub-group looking at the theory of the national economy, with theorists and no-one else discussing theoretical problems; and another sub-group on statistics, in which statisticians and other experts on statistics and no-one else will discuss problems of their own choosing. Experts could also consult other interested parties, but, if they so desired, limit participation in discussions to active members who have technical knowledge and the perspective of a real specialist. In addition, the mother Society will conduct its meeting in the same way as now, but limit publications to the prepared themes of the works of the Society. In this way, the Society will place the main emphasis of its activities on *publications*.

I now need to speak about what works the Society will in this way take up with the specialists in the largest possible circle of co-workers who will want to work with us and place themselves, with us, at the service of the issue. It is understood that these comments here can provide only the broadest sketch – if you wish, they are a mere *feuilleton*,[3] or review of the topic. After all, gentlemen, the formulation of the issue; the *statement of the problem* to work on, is our decisive scientific task.

Gentlemen, the first theme that the Society has deemed it possible to take up in a purely scientific way is a *sociology of journalism*. We cannot disguise from ourselves the fact that it is a colossal theme, which demands not only very significant financial backing for the preparatory work but also that it will be impossible for us to deal with the opportunity appropriately without the co-operation of the leading lights of journalism and those who have the greatest trust in our Society and goodwill towards our objectives. It will also be impossible if representatives of the newspaper publishers or the journalists we meet do not trust the Society to realize its objectives, or if they believe that we will make moral criticisms of the prevailing situation in the press. Without the cooperation of those with interests in journalism, I say, it will be impossible for us to reach our goal. In the near future, the committee responsible for the task will try to get a group of journalism specialists together, and another group of journalism theorists – who already exist in large numbers. We already know of brilliant theoretical publications in this area (just for a moment, let me remind you of the book by Löbl,[4] especially because it is much less well known than it deserves) – and we would even like to win over practising journalists as co-workers. Based on the previous tentative proceedings, there is hope that when we turn – as we will in the very near future – to the large newspaper publishers and to the associations of newspaper publishers and the newspaper editors, they will extend their goodwill to us. If this does not happen, the Society would sooner avoid having a meeting than hold one from which nothing is likely to result.

Gentlemen, there is no purpose in saying anything here about the great general significance of the press. In view of what has already been said about those periodicals of high standing, it would cause me to fall under the suspicion of flattering the representatives of the press. If the press has been compared with commanding generals – it is certainly only said by the foreign press—so everyone knows that there is nothing left on earth to which we can compare them and we would have to look heavenwards for comparisons. I simply

3 In his account of the Society's work in this paper, Weber uses the term *feuilleton*, meaning the part of a European newspaper carrying reviews, serialized fiction, games and crosswords, and so on, or a review or article in a *feuilleton*.

4 Weber means the Viennese newspaperman, Emil Löbl, whose book *Kultur und Presse*, a theoretical work, so impressed him (see Weber, 1998: 1021).

remind you: think for a moment what modern life would be without the kind of publicity the press creates. Honoured guests, antiquity also had its publicity. Jakob Burkhardt stood with dread regarding the scrutiny of the Hellenistic public life, which included consideration of the whole life of Athenian citizens, down to the most intimate details. This type of scrutiny no longer exists, and it is rather interesting to ask how does publicity look today, and how is it to look in the future? What is made public through the newspaper *and what is not*? If 150 years ago the English Parliament forced journalists to their knees to make an apology because of a breach of privilege[5] that contravened parliamentary limits in the reporting of proceedings, today, a mere threat not to print a member's speech forces Parliament to its knees, the function of parliament-arianism has obviously changed, as has the function of the press. At the same time, *local* differences must exist. For example, the American Stock Exchange covered its windows with milk glass, so that the movements of stocks and shares could not be communicated by some signal to the outside world. At the same time, almost all the essential characteristics of newspaper composition are necessarily influenced by the exchange publications.

As is well known, we do not ask what *should* be made public. Opinions differ widely on that subject, as everyone knows. However, it would naturally be interesting to find out which opinions on particular subjects are contemporary and which were held in the past, and by whom. That falls inside our sphere of investigation – but only questions which, like these, are based on fact. Every-one knows that in England, for example, people hold different opinions from us Germans. This is evidenced when some English lord marries an American woman: a circular (*Steckbrief*) is published in the American press regarding the physical and the mental traits and all that goes with them – which naturally includes the dowry. By contrast, a reputable German newspaper would follow German public opinion, which is one of disdain for such matters. Where does the difference come from? If, in Germany today, we have decided that in the case of the most serious stories, affecting the most serious representatives of the press corps, purely personal matters are to be excluded from newspaper publicity – what are the reasons and what are the results? On the other hand, a socialist publicist, Anton Menger,[6] was of the opinion that in the state of the future, the press will have the opposite task: matters that cannot be brought before the criminal court will be subjected to a form of trial by press; the press will have taken over the old role of the censor. It would be a worthwhile task to determine what the *Weltanschauung* [world view] that is behind these two

5 Weber uses the English 'breach of privilege'.

6 Menger (1841–1906) was a Viennese civil rights professor who wrote on socio-political questions.

stances. Clearly, this *alone* is our task; it is not our role to take up a position in support of one or the other.

Above all, we will have to investigate the *power* relations created by newspaper publicity. Essentially, these have less significance in the case of scientific achievement than that for something like show business or a director's performance, which are transient. It is especially significant that what is read into a newspaper article – the meaning gleaned from reading between the lines – generally has the greatest effect. In a certain sense, newspaper theatre and also literature reviewers can most easily make or destroy a person. For each section of a newspaper, beginning with the political pages, these power relations are extremely different. A newspaper's relationships with political parties, with the business world, with all the countless figures who influence the public, with the groups they have influenced and their interested parties – an enormous sphere of influence – all appear today for the first time among the elements of structured sociological work. But let us come to the particular starting point of this investigation.

As we approach the press sociologically, it is fundamental to recognize that the press today is necessarily a capitalistic, private business venture; but at the same time, the press has a very strange position by comparison with any other business in that it has two entirely different types of customers. People who buy the newspaper are one type, and these may be the masses of subscribers or of single buyers – these trends are different in every region or country where the newspaper is sold. The advertisers are the second type, and between these two groups of consumers there exists a strange dynamic of changing relationships (*Wechselbeziehungen*). For example, it is certainly important for a newspaper to have many advertisers, if it has many subscribers and, in a limited sense, also the reverse. But the advertisers do not only have a role in the budget of the press. They have a bigger role than the subscribers, but another way of stating the case is to say that a newspaper can never have too many advertisers, yet, in contrast to sellers of other goods, it can have too many buyers. This is because when the current print-run is sold out, it is not possible to raise the price to cover the cost of increasing the size of the issue. That is one of the most serious problems for certain types of newspapers and, in general, the result is that after a specific number of copies sold, the newspaper has no further interest in expanding the size of the issue or, at least, it *can* come to that if it is difficult to further increase the advertising rates. That is peculiar to the press, and although it is purely a business matter, it obviously has wider consequences. To make international comparisons, there is a very great difference in the degree and type of connection between the press, which wants to inform the public about political and other issues and to give the facts, and to attract advertising in accordance with the advertising demand of the business world; namely, if one compares Germany to France. Why? What are the general consequences of these differences? These questions have been written about so often, that we must now take them up, because only partial concurrence of opinions has been established.

We go farther: an outstanding modern feature of the press is the growth of the capital *demand* for newspaper publishers. The question is, to what extent does the growing capital demand signify a growing monopoly of the established publishers? The question is not yet decided, and is being argued over by the best-trained specialists. The answer may depend on differing circumstances, for it can be seen from an effect of the growing capital demand that the monopoly of the established newspapers is of differing strengths, depending on whether a particular publisher relies on subscriptions or on sales from street vendors – as in those countries where every single day one has the choice to buy a paper different from the one that he bought the day before. This would seem to make it easier to introduce new papers. *Perhaps* that is something to investigate; and if so, an answer to the question requires that information about the growing capital demand must be combined with an investigation into its effects: does this growing standing capital also signify rising power marked by an estimate of public opinion? Or, is the reverse true, as is maintained but not yet clearly proven – the growing vulnerability of individual firms in the face of vacillating public opinion? The conspicuous changes of editorial opinion of certain French newspapers have been singled out for comment in this context. An example is the effect of the Dreyfus affair on *Le Figaro*. It is easy to see the size of the capital invested in the modern newspaper publisher as set against some similar public disagreement, which the public make clear in cancellations, which in turn makes the company increasingly nervous and thus more dependent on the public, without which it could not remain in business. Obviously in France, with sales from newspaper vendors dominating, the facility to make great editorial changes will naturally fall as the readership grows. That means that the consequences of the growing capital demand are connected to a rising dependence on each of those daily fluxes. Is that true? That is a question we have to pose. It is something that specialists in the press maintain – I am not one – but it is disputed by those who are.

Furthermore, how do we perhaps stand in the wake of a possible increase in the fixed capital for newspaper production, perhaps resulting from the growing demand for capital for a pool of journalists? What is the likely outcome? Gentlemen, that has been disputed by the most energetic of specialists of all stripes, from theorists to professionals in the field. However, a major representative of this opinion, Lord Northcliffe, could know better than anyone, for he is one of the greatest newspaper magnates there has ever been. What would be the result for the character of a newspaper if this happened? A mere glance, shows that today's newspapers, from the greatest to those that merely exist, have widely differing characters. Enough! I only use examples to show how the business character of newspaper publishing houses must be taken into consideration – we must ask ourselves: what does capitalist development *within* journalism signify for the sociological position of the press in general, and for its role in the development of public opinion?

Another problem: The institutional character of the modern press in Germany has a specific expression in that the sources for the information that appears in the press are not revealed. A great deal has been said for and against this aspect of the press. We take no position; but rather, ask: *How is it,* for example, that to maintain the anonymity of sources is a feature of the German press, while in other countries, such as France, it is less important, and England is closer to us. Today in France there is only one single newspaper that imposes a strict policy of anonymity of sources: *Le Temps.* In England there are many newspapers like *The Times,* which maintain strict rules about protecting the names of their sources. There can be many entirely different reasons. It can be – as it, for example, appears to be the case with *The Times* – that the persons from whom the newspaper gets its information are often so highly placed that it would not be possible for them publicly to give information under their names. Elsewhere, however, the reasons for the policy may be the entirely the opposite. The policy therefore depends on this: how does the question appear from the standpoint of conflicts of interest, once these exist – and this is unavoidable – between the interests of individual journalists in becoming well known, and the interests of the newspaper, which cannot allow itself to become dependent on the co-operation of any particular journalist. Obviously, business interests throw a very differently light on the subject, depending on whether street sales dominate or not. Above all, the characters of people (*Volkseigenart*) involved in politics play a part – as in a nation like Germany, for example, whose people are more inclined to be impressed by the institutional power of a 'supra-individual' journal than by the opinion of a single individual. The people of other countries may be free from metaphysics of this type.

Questions like these really lead on to the area of freelance journalism; which is expressed in entirely different ways in Germany than in France, where the freelance journalist is universal, as is the situation in England. The question must therefore be asked: who from the world outside journalism would write for today's publications, and what would they write? Also, who would not write and what would they decline to write? That leads to another general question:

how does the press generally acquire the material it offers to the public? In general, what does it offer the public? Has Germany experienced a continuous growth of exclusively *factual* newspapers? That has happened in Britain, the USA and Germany in complete contrast with France – because what the French primarily want is a fashionable, up-to-date newspaper. Why? An American, for example, wants nothing from his newspaper other than facts. In general, he considers that it is not worth the trouble of reading opinions about the facts that are publicized in the press. For, as a supporter of democracy, he is convinced that in principle he understands the facts as well as, if not better than the journalists who write for the newspaper. The Frenchman also wants to be democratic. Where, therefore, is the difference? In any case, the social function of the newspaper is entirely different in both countries.

Despite these differences, the budget of the news service provided by the press in all of the countries of the earth is increasingly burdensome, looming more and more into the foreground. We must therefore enquire into this. Our final question is: who, in particular, are the ultimate sources of the news – can they be traced to the international connections of the large news bureaux? Important work needs to be done on this, but a beginning has been made already. The assertions that have already been made in this area contradict one another in some ways, and it would be helpful to obtain more material than is achievable today, if it proves possible to do that while maintaining objectivity.

Yet insofar as the contents of a newspaper are neither the news nor, on the other hand, the regurgitation of clichéd advertisements – there are, as is known, mass repetitions of the contents of press releases, from the sport-and-puzzle corner to the novel, which are selected from among all the possibilities available to some large publishers – I say that as long as the press is not crammed with clichéd publicity or with news, what is generally offered today by individual journalists to us in Germany at least, by contrast with many non-German countries, is still of fundamental significance for the assessment of a newspaper. We could not now be content with the products already under consideration but must give proper attention to their producers and enquire about their fate and the situations of their journalists. It is now the fate, for example, of the German journalist, to have an entirely heterogeneous appeal to those from abroad. In England, there are journalists and other newspaper people who, under certain circumstances, sit in the Upper House of Parliament, men who, for the most part, had no other calling than as businessmen,[7] who perform brilliantly for the political party to which they belong and underbid all others – may I, in this case only, not say 'overbid' – in the creation of commercial newspapers.

7 Weber uses the term 'businessmen' in English.

In France, journalists have become ministers in large numbers. By contrast, in Germany this happens only as a rare exception. Wholly aside from these striking examples, we should also ask how the relations of professional journalists have changed in the recent past in different countries.

What makes a journalist – what educational background do journalists need, and what are the vocational demands on a modern journalist? Also, what is the vocational path of German journalists in comparison to foreign journalists and what, ultimately, are the possibly extra-vocational opportunities for a journalist to earn a living (*Lebenschancen*) in general today in Germany and abroad? The general situation of the journalist is, as everyone knows, very different when considered in relation to politics, the character of the newspaper, etc. For example, the socialist press and the Catholic press occupy a special niche and must be treated differently from other sectors of the press.

Finally, what *effects* on us come from our investigation of the created product which the completed newspaper presents? There is an enormous literature on that subject and most of it is very worthwhile, but much of it comes from superior specialists, who often reveal the sharpest contradictions. Gentlemen, it is well known that the effects of journalism on the brain have been directly enquired into. Investigation is needed into the consequences of the circumstances that modern man has become used to: that before he goes to his daily work, he consumes a ragout,[8] which forces him to fit into a certain kind of framework that permeates all areas of cultural life, beginning with the political and continuing to the theatre and all other possible areas. It is apparent that these are not equally weighted. It is also appropriate and easy to make general comments about what emerges from the influences to which modern man is exposed. It is not easy to work on the problem in its earliest and simplest stages.

The next question will most likely be: what type of newspaper has modern man become accustomed to? All possible theories have been put forward in answer to that. One maintained that books have been crowded out because of the newspaper. This is a possibility. Looked at quantitatively, German book production is blossoming as in no other country. Nowhere else in the world are so many titles cast out on to the market than by us. However, the numbers of volumes printed of these same books show the reverse. In Russia, before freedom of the press was introduced, editions of 20,000 to 30,000 copies were printed – with great respect for the character of Anton Menger, unbelievable books such as his *Neue Sittenlehre* (*New Doctrine of Morals*) were published. High-circulation newspapers attempted a search for the fundamental, 'final' philosophical idea. That would be impossible in Germany, and in Russia it

---

8 By 'ragout', Weber means a newspaper that has bits of everything.

would be impossible under the influence of the least comparative freedom of the press, the beginnings of which are already appearing.

The press has brought about an unquestionably powerful change in reading habits, and with that a powerful displacement of the nature, of the whole way in which modern man receives information from outside. The continuing changes and the understanding of these massive changes of public opinion, from all universal and inexhaustible possibilities, standpoints and interests, place an enormous weight on the character of modern man. But how? That is something we have to investigate.

I cannot allow myself to express this and close, without noting that we have finally to investigate the press in the following ways. First, what does it contribute to the character of modern man? Second: How are objective, supra-individual cultural values influenced, what is rejected and what is destroyed by mass beliefs, mass hopes, and new feelings for life (*Lebensgefühlen*) that at one moment may be utterly destroyed and then created anew. Those are the final questions that we have posed and you will see immediately, honoured guests, that the way to answer such questions is extraordinarily time-consuming.

So you now ask what will we need to carry out such research and where will it come from? The newspapers are the material we need to work on and we will now, as we have clearly said we will, begin mechanically to question and to measure, using scissors and compass, how in the course of the last generation the contents of newspapers have altered in a quantitative sense, not least in the advertising, in the *feuilleton* (the leisure section, which contains no news), between *feuilleton* and lead article, between lead article and news, between what is generally used to obtain the news and what is no longer used today. All those areas have changed extraordinarily and the investigations that seek to confirm this are now in their earliest stages.

From these quantitative investigations we will move to the qualitative. We will explain newspaper styles, typesetting, the problems that affect the content of a newspaper and the external problems, the apparent repressing of emotions in a newspaper, on which its existence always rests, and many other aspects of newspapers and journalism. Finally, we hope to approach the answer to the wide-ranging question: of what benefit are newspapers to us?

Gentlemen, I must now express myself essentially still more briefly and sketchily to set out two other problem areas, which, in addition, the Society intends to address.

The second theme that I must first necessarily formulate is broadly this: that it is a fundamental task of any society for sociology to draw a picture of the object of its work that is conventionally labelled 'social'; that means, what lies between the organized, political or other recognized powers such as state power, the powers of the local political community (*Gemeinde*), and the official church, and the naturally evolved community or *Gemeinschaft* of the family? Above all, a *sociology of the essence of the association* (*Vereinswesens*) in the broadest sense of the word, beginning with bowling club (*Kegelklub*)[9] and going on – let us say it forcefully – to political parties and to religious, artistic or literary sects.

Gentlemen, even such an enormous theme is disguised under the most diverse points of view in the most diverse statements of the problem, at least a few of which I can indicate quite quickly.

Unquestionably, the contemporary person is, in addition to much else, an association person (*Vereinsmensch*) to a terrible, unanticipated, degree. This cannot be overestimated, since 'Association-Relief' (*Vereins-Enthebungs*) organizations have been formed. In this respect, Germany has set a very high standard. The facts can be determined from any arbitrarily selected official list of local associations – even if it only lists most of the associations, and that is usually not the case, and in reality may never happen, although the official list for Berlin, to pick an example, is incomplete by comparison with those of smaller cities. For instance, cities of 30,000 inhabitants have some 300 different associations; so that an association exists for every 100 inhabitants – that is, for every 20 heads of families.

Gentlemen, quantitative distribution does not always go hand-in- hand with qualitative significance. Which country qualifies as 'association-land' (*Vereinsland*) *par excellence?* It is without doubt, America, because there, for the middle classes, the membership of some associations leads directly to legitimization as a gentleman. It is more accurate to say that today 'europeanization' belongs to everything. A pair of extreme examples: first, a German nose specialist told me that his first client in Cincinnati had said to him before the examination began: 'I belong to the First Baptist Church in so-and-so street'.[10] What that had to do with the nasal problem, the doctor could not fathom. It meant nothing more than: 'I am a patented gentleman – and I pay well and promptly'. The second patient who came to him began by showing him a type of honorary legionnaire's rosette in his lapel. The doctor enquired about it and learned that it was the emblem of a club that would vote a person in only after a careful investigation into his personality, so anyone who belonged to it was legitimatized as 'a gentleman'. There is an abundant distribution of this type of club and of associations of every other type. Today, they are increasing worldwide.

All associations originated from one type, which is really best studied in America – the *sect* in the full sense of the word, historic or modern. A sect is an

---

9 For a discussion of *Kegelklub* and its negative connotations, see the Introduction.
10 Weber has 'First Baptist-church', in English.

association of specifically qualified men and is not an institution, because, according to sociological structural principles, it rejects the sanction of authoritarian associations (*Zwangsverbände*) such as state and church – so that it *must* be an association. In America, it therefore has the role of certifier of the social qualifications, so to speak, of businessmen. For example, before the Baptists accept someone as a member, he has to submit to a test, one that reminds us of our Reserve Officer's test, which covers his entire past: visits to drinking places, relationships with women, card games played, bank accounts and all unpaid accounts, and examines all aspects of personal conduct before he can be permitted to be baptized. The person who is then baptized is legitimatized as unconditionally creditworthy and a good deal-maker.

Other traditional American associations do the same, not quite as strictly, but in a similar way and with similar consequences. Free-masonry functions entirely similarly – and so it does in Germany, as any Freemason will readily confirm, but the effect is strongest in America. I was once told by a man who really bemoaned the fact that, for external reasons, he could not attain the position of Chair Master. To my question, why was it important to him? He said: 'When I am Chair Master and go on business trips, I can come forward with the secret signal, and so I can get all of the customers, I can sell every item of my stock because there everyone presumes that I offer only honest goods at honest prices. Had I not at some time proven myself, the Freemasons would not have tolerated me in their midst.' Such is the way business life operates in general in America. Whoever is not accepted there – for example, the German American is seldom lucky enough to be accepted – does not attain a position of importance.

Democracy in America is not a sand pile, but an entanglement of exclusive sects, associations and clubs. These support the selection of those who fit into American life in general, support them, in that they help them in business and politics, and into every position of authority (*Herrschaft*) in social life. How is it in Germany? Are there analogies? If so, of what type and to what extent? Where do they occur? And what are the consequences? Where are they not found, and why?

All these questions relate to associations as looked at from outside. A second question is: how does the membership of a particular type of association work from inside? It can be said in general that the person who belongs to an association, be it, for example, a *Couleur* in Germany, or a Greek-letter Society or other student club in America,[11] must, with his fellow members

11 A *Couleur* was a German student association that had its own colours, hence the name. Weber uses the English 'Greek-letter Society', as fraternities and sororities in US universities were originally called.

(*Verbandsgenossen*) *assert* himself vis-à-vis both the outside world and inside the association? The question is: how does he assert himself? In the examples given, this depends on, for example, which ideal of manliness (*Männlichkeit*) is practised consciously and intentionally, or, alternatively, unconsciously and traditionally, in a German *Couleur*, an English sports club or an American student association. The conditions under which a member might win the respect (*Achtung*)[12] of his fellows are naturally fundamentally different. They exist so that in each country and in the various levels of society, classes, and categories of associations, the individual can be consciously or unconsciously selected and then groomed, as it were, for membership, according to the prevailing ideal. What matters is not just the question of whether the prospective member gains the outward respect of his fellows; we must always ask how the individual who has been exposed to these influences lives up to his own ideal, over and above his own self-respect and his desire to be a person of note. What shifts of the inner position and outer balances of what we call 'personality' could be necessary in order to reconcile the two? Because as the individual seeks to resolve the conflict by responding to the influences of the social milieu in which he finds himself, the inner 'I', his feeling of self-worth may need to be shifted on to fundamentally different bases to comply with the social situation.

To continue. Every association to which one belongs is based on relationships of dominance (*Herrschaft*) among men. First, at least according to the association's unwritten rules, the relationships are formally and officially dominated by a majority. For this reason, what stands in question is the psychology of the dominant majority over the individual, and in these private associations, that psychological mechanism can be seen to work in a very specific way. Here, then, I make only the following, definitive, point: that clearly in any body that carries authority, whether it be called a party, association, club, or any other name, in reality the dominance always lies with a dominant minority, which may occasionally be a dictator. One person may come into a position of dominance in the process of selection for and adaptation to the work of the society, in which one person appears to be most capable, and who, as a result, eventually gains a dominant position in the association.

How and under what conditions, I would like to ask, under which rules of play (*Spielregeln*) is this selection of leaders made inside individual associations, parties, etc., which is decisive for the question of which type of personality achieves a position of dominance? That is a question that can only be answered by taking into consideration the cultural conditions of the environment in

---

12 *Achtung* can mean 'respect' or 'attention'.

which the association operates. This is an important question, central to sociological investigation, and no less important is one that has a connection with it: which methods does the leading group use, other than its own dominance, to secure loyalty? There are already many important preliminary works on this question.

Furthermore, what types of relations exist between an association, regardless of which type – political party, etc., down to a bowling club (*Kegelklub*) – and something that may be termed (however, paradoxical this may seem) *Weltanschauung* or 'world view'. A relationship of this nature is somehow present where least expected, albeit in very different ways. First, it is an everyday occurrence that those associations that emerged from the great ideas of *Weltanschauung* become mechanisms, which, although they grow, let the ideas on which they were founded ebb away. That belongs simply to what may be generally seen as the tragic reality of attempting to put great ideas into practice. To every association belongs some apparatus, however modest, that as soon as the association becomes propagandish, and that the apparatus is in some manner revealed and is taken over by the *vocational* humanity.[13]

Consider – to take a great example – the delicate and thorny (*heikles*) problem area of erotic life. The propaganda of ideas in this area has already become a *pecuniary* foundation of existence. I do not speak here in moral reproach against the persons concerned, and I myself hold to the conviction that it is not right that many professors use the lectern as an outlet for publicizing their subjective political or other ideas. Yet it is a fact and it clearly has very wide-ranging consequences when the stage is reached where ideas become manifest and where the spread of those ideas is the basis for material existence – although the consequences are naturally different, depending on the type and character of the idea. On the other hand, gentlemen, almost every association attracts even those who in principle wish to shun it, and this in itself contains moderation of *Weltanschauung* (*Weltanschauungsmäßige*). In a certain sense, one could maintain this: that a German bowling club, in a greater degree even in a German singing group – gentlemen, to maintain my theme – the bloom of the singing associations in Germany exhibit, in my opinion, observable effects even in areas where one would not expect them – in the political arena, for example. A person who daily experiences the streaming out of powerful sensitivities from his breast through the larynx, without any relation to his actions, without an adequate acting out of these expressed powerful feelings in powerful activities – and that is the essence of the singing association – that is a person who, in summary, is easily a 'good citizen' in the passive sense of the

---

13 *Berufs' Menschentum*. Weber's point seems to be that the association becomes more 'professional'.

term. It is no wonder that the monarchy has so great a preference for that type of institution. 'Where one sings, one can rest'; but there, great strong passions and strong actions are missing.[14] It sounds paradoxical, it is perhaps, I admit, rather one-sided that it should also be no rebuke – perhaps it can be a standpoint from which the thought can even be expressed that this is the realm of riches of the German people, who are capable of drawing fully of this solution and on that basis create its own artistic culture. It is possible to go further and say that *every* type in the introduction from hindrances between reception and expression finds its basis. I leave it there, for anything that touches on the question of value is none of *our* business. I maintain only that relationships of the type I have indicated are possible – I do not know how strongly, and I may have exaggerated – and *can* exist.

In such and similar cases the unconscious influences of the entire habitus allow themselves to be essentially treated through the content of the activities of the association. But, there are the totally different shadings in the type of over-reaching of pure factual or pure real goals in the pursuit of communities in the area of influence and regimenting of the practical conduct of life. It can also result from the fully conscious; it can come from the pure factual, real positions, from behind which we would have never suspected. Consider that most medical and psychological theories are openly directed towards the building of sects. One particular theory of a famous Viennese psychiatrist led to the creation of a sect, which has already spread so far that anyone who is not connected with the theories is strictly excluded.[15] A person free from 'complexes' is the ideal, and a way of life through which such a person is created and can be maintained is the object of this sect. The regimentation stemming from this idea affects every branch of life – yet no one who first considers this theory from a purely psychiatric point of view, for scientific purposes, could construe that this might be the result, although the connection is very easily understood.

The same can be said for example about the area of aesthetics: the formation of artistic sects that carry the feeling of the artistic world. From a sociological point of view, that feeling is of the highest interest. What they possess is very similar to the religious sects – to have in incarnation of the deities – I remind you of Stefan George's sect[16] – the rules governing the

14 Weber's point is that a person who is a member of an association uses it as an emotional outlet. The member of the German singing group uses song to express powerful emotion and feelings that otherwise might have found an outlet in political activity. Because the German singing associations are an outlet for such feelings, the authorities approve of them.

15 Meaning Sigmund Freud.

16 Stefan George (1868–1933) was a poet and writer, the founder and centre of a dedicated group of artistic intellectuals who believed in a community based on new aesthetic principles. While Weber disapproved of this, George was a frequent visitor to the Weber house in Heidelberg.

practical conduct of life, the inner attitude to life formulated by the sect for their disciples can be really wide-ranging. The same experience can be observed in the area of racial theoreticians. Marriage according to the noble genealogical tree can clearly be replaced by marriage determined by hygienic genealogical charts. And as everyone knows, a sect may be formed for this noble purpose by both esoteric and exoteric disciples. I use the word 'sect' in this talk in a *totally value-free* manner. This expression is particularly notorious for us because, it ties us to the concept of narrowness, although entirely without foundation. Sharply defined ideals cannot be brought to life in any other way than initially by the formation of a sect of enthusiastic followers, who strive to realize their ideals and therefore band together and separate from others.

Gentlemen, I must break off so as not to put too much of a claim on your time. We come finally to two statements on major problems like those of the press. How do the various categories of clubs and associations work, beginning with political parties – for these can either be [political] machines, pure [political] machines, like American political parties, or parties that supposedly have a *Weltanschauung* like today's Social Democratic Party, which really believes it has a world view although in fact it has long since stopped having one; or political parties that really do have a *Weltanschauung*, most of which are still mainly parties of the centre.[17] There also exist all the different pairings of ideas and mechanisms – and, as I say, how do they influence cultural values in both types – the single individual and the objective, supra-individual cultural values?

If you now ask about the material with which such an investigation should be conducted, so it is with the material that must first be asked about. Again, it is with the totally dry, and trivial, and without such dry, trivial matter even with much money and with much work-power not much will come from it. What will pay first is to hold the systematic inquiry into the associations in order to determine which vocations, which geographical, ethnic, and social origins of its members. I do not exclude the possibility, if also even if I am not certain, that in the course of time a register of the most important categories of associations of this type could be formed so that the principle of selection could be determined. It is this principle of selection that is naturally mostly unconscious and will be discovered only by gathering the greatest and most comprehensive material. In this way, we will have what we need to analyse the

---

17 Weber differentiates among three types of political parties. First, the American political party which functions solely as a machine without any idealistic view; second, the German party that pretends that it has an idealistic view but in reality left it for political reality, and third, those German political parties which maintain some idealistic view. Several points need to be made here: Weber is not endorsing or denigrating any of these three types but is only sketching a sociology of political parties. Further, this is not to be taken as an exhaustive discussion but only a hint.

effects of the association from inside, from the members, from outside, in terms of its effects on the outside world and how those effects are achieved – and all from a new, sociological perspective. Work for many years!

Since I have just spoken about 'selection', I mention in this connection our completion of the planning stages of a large area of work. That has been done by Professor Eulenburg in Leipzig, who is with us to discuss his systematic work on the exciting question of selection for the leading vocations in modern society – those vocations that are usually known as 'leading' – as if sociology can start from anything other than the conventional – that is, the leading economic and political professional, the scientific, literary, artistic, and spiritual leaders, the leading official, teacher, entrepreneur, etc. We would like to enquire into where these people come from, who were their fathers and grandfathers, what are their ethnic backgrounds, what has been their life story – that is to say, what hurdles have they jumped over to reach the position they now occupy; in short, how, in general, has the process of selection worked? All this we can naturally discover only by studying large numbers of people in these positions, so that we must use all the ethnic, vocational, social, etc. material, to which we have access, which provides us with the best opportunities to find out about these vocations and positions. This is a task, which, once again can possibly be accomplished in the course of time by a comprehensive survey.

Gentlemen, I have in the time given to me simply tried to make clear to you through carefully chosen, *purely illustrative*, examples, that in certain accessible problem areas there are questions that are worth scientific investigation.

You can already see that these concrete tasks that I have mentioned here are not of the type that would allow you to count on seeing brilliant results in the next year. The Society must have patience, as must the public. These tasks demand not only the selflessness of submission to a limited goal – something that is seldom encountered today – but as these goals increase in number, they require – regrettably, I must add – *very considerable pecuniary means*. Gentlemen, for the purpose of the press investigation alone, the costs for the preliminary work are estimated to be approximately 25,000 Marks. Of these 25,000 Marks, we now have the use of 20,000 Marks through an agreement with the Heidelberg Academy of Science and with the Institute for the Common Good here in Frankfurt, and private contributions from inside and outside our Society. It is to be hoped that the necessary remainder will also be contributed in some way from the private sector, because under no circumstances will we begin our work before we are certain that the funding we consider necessary will be enough and will have been put at our disposal. The money for the other investigations does not as yet exist, other than the on-going funds of the

Society, and, with a membership of little more than 200, these are not enough to finance such work. While we hope that the membership increases, I say that the continuing resources of the Society can certainly not be used to support these tasks. They must be used, at least in the main, for the day-to-day business of the Society and to help carry the costs of conferences like this one. As has been said, in future we intend to support them in an essentially altered and better form.

Thus, we are, as we openly confess, dependent on patronage – on a patronage that has already manifested itself in what is an unusual way in Germany. For, gentlemen, in total contrast to the situation not just in America but in general in foreign countries, it is extremely rare in Germany to raise money for purely scientific activities. There is money for the problems of technology, perhaps for the problems of aviation, and perhaps something for the precious body and its cure – for radiotherapy, therefore, or similar technologies that are likely to produce therapeutic results in the long term. There are fortunately also increasing funds for artistic purposes. When we in Germany are given money for scientific purposes, in general we can be certain that it is with the state's interest. This comes from reasons that I will not elaborate upon here, by the very different manner and certainly subjectively reporting of it, yet it is objective in my opinion, but it is not always reported in an agreeable manner. Having said that, and with all the respect due to the state for everything it does for us, by contrast with the situation in other countries, it is obviously not enough in the long term for the progress of science.

Until now there has been only *one* city that in large measure practises patronage for the furtherance of science and which *excludes* state intervention of any type, as is the norm in America, and that is Frankfurt am Main. It is not possible to find out whether Frankfurt am Main will be able to continue this. Instead, one must hope – and this depends not only on our special scientific work but also on the progress of scientific work in general – that at least the brilliant names in the field of German pure science have become household names. To achieve that assumes a patronage that will have the patience to wait until the science will somehow finally 'serve life'. I say that one must hope that a similar patronage outside that one city will also mature in Germany in larger measure than has been the case; and, as has been said, not just to further the special tasks of this Society; but the interests of scientific work in general.

(Lively applause.)

[Close of morning session by the Chairman, Professor Tönnies:

The order of the day for our morning session is exhausted. The second session of today will begin this afternoon at 4pm, and Professor Sombart is to give a lecture on 'Technology and Culture'. The session is thus recessed until this afternoon.

The session closed at 12:30pm.]

WERNER SOMBART
Technology and Culture

[Thursday Afternoon, 20 October 1910
Opening address by the Chairman, Professor Tönnies:

Honoured assembled members, today's session of the first sociology
conference is continued. I give the floor to Professor Dr Werner Sombart,
for his lecture.]

The broad conception of my theme of 'Technology and Culture' naturally
makes it necessary to give it an entirely general treatment; and in order for this
entirely general treatment to have some success, I have planned to treat it in an
essentially methodological-programmatic-problematic-dispositionary manner.
That means that I would like to give you a few examples to answer the question:
What is the significance of placing 'and' between the words 'technology' and
'culture'? My speech – my lecture – will be, then, in three parts: two short parts,
in which I will speak first on technology as I conceive of it; and second, on the
concept of culture; and for the third and longer part I will offer an analysis of
the little word 'and'.

In the broadest sense of the word 'technology', we could use any procedures, any part or combination of parts and all systems, of any degree of
complexity, to achieve a specified goal with it. In this broadest sense there
could be, for example, a technology of song, a technology of speaking, a
technology of war, a technology of flight, a technology of speech, a technology
of drama – indeed there is supposedly even a technology of love, the *ars amandi*
(art of love) of the ancients. However, when we speak of technology and culture
as a theme of a lecture, we clearly mean something narrower and, by implica-
tion, the use of particular methods or the application of specific resources to a
specific object or objects in order to reach a specific goal. If, for example, we

speak of a technology of medical operations, we mean first the entire procedure the surgeon applies to a patient; but second, in a narrower sense, we mean the employment of specific instruments, antiseptic agents and the like.

Technology is always concerned with the employment of an instrument, if I may be permitted to say so, and instruments can, in turn, be used in the most varied ways: instruments for music; instruments for warfare; instruments for removing teeth, etc. An instrument always pushes itself into the procedure. I therefore, name this technology 'the technology of instruments'.

Yet even this is not the concept of technology that we have particularly in mind when we speak of technology and culture, but rather something even narrower: namely, all the procedures that go into the manufacture of instruments generally, including all the goods that go into their manufacture, their production. This is production technology, or 'economic technology', because here economy and technology are in conjunction. In fact, this technology can fulfil demands that spring from the needs of the economy. It is primary technology, i.e. it is the basis of all other technologies insofar as almost all technologies are instrumental, in that most of the goods they produce serve to secure a particular result. A brief examination shows that this economic or production technology is primary technology, as opposed to other, secondary, technologies. Transport technology is secondary technology. Flight technology is secondary technology because it is made possible through the production of aluminium, engines in particular, the use of specific gases, and the manufacture of other materials. In the end, all technology goes back to the formation of production technology, which I therefore call 'primary technology'.

Technology encompasses skill and knowledge. That, one allows, is generally known, for with all technology there has to be a detailed knowledge – of the materials involved in its production, the power of which it is capable, its nature and the applications to which it can be put. On the other hand, all technology involves a particular skill – perhaps a known skill, as in the use of a tool.

Now it is not so easy to pin down the concept of culture and because of that I would prefer not to try to say what culture is. I have at least not attempted to define the concept. I find it less important to say what culture is than to say how culture expresses itself. That is sufficient for our purposes.

I am therefore going to continue by remarking that culture appears in one of culture's possessions – in the possession of cultural goods. These cultural goods may be ideal or material in nature: material when they are to be used in creating a cultural act. Goods are used in every cultural act, yet we speak of a 'material culture', in which goods are created entirely for the cultural act. For example, goods may be created to satisfy our need for nourishment, clothing, housing, jewellery, comfort, and so on, while ideal cultural goods are always available as a factual substrate, but they are entirely symbolic of a particular cultural act.

Again, this ideal culture is a very different type of culture, as is commonly known. Thus it is concerned with what might be termed institutional culture – the possession of human organizations, state organizations, church organizations, customs (*Sitten*) organizations, economic organizations, etc. Insofar as there is real possession of goods of this type, as I said, the natures of these organizations are ideal, but they have a factual substrate: for example, all state legislation is bound to certain constitutional instruments. Under certain circumstances this can entirely disappear; yet after a millennium it may be recovered – as in the case of the Aristotelian Constitution. It can then grow into a new form, into a new ideal form. Having risen from the factual substrate, its significance is obviously entirely different from goods that are manufactured, for example, the coats we wear.

Immaterial culture, spiritual culture embraces all the cultural goods we possess – scientific knowledge, for example, artistic production, world views (*Weltanschauungen*), ideals, strivings, values, would belong here. And all these cultural goods and cultural possessions could be gathered together and labeled 'objective culture', or better, 'objectifying culture', because it is a supra-individual culture – that is, its existence has no connection with the individual, and in this it differs from 'personal' culture, the second largest type of culture.

'Personal' culture manifests itself in the living individual. It is born with each individual and dies when that individual dies. It is physical type: the development of the body. It is ideal type: the cultivation of the soul. These die – that is the determining point – when the individual who possesses them dies, while all other cultural goods outlive the individual.

Besides these two large groups in which culture manifests itself, a third may be differentiated, whose attributes are not entirely covered by the other two. It could be called 'cultural style' – a wholly specific 'cut' of culture. The existence of this third group cannot be entirely proved, or is not as demonstrable as certain goods or attributes of 'objective' culture, or an individual who is adapted to some particular culture. Nevertheless, we suppose it to be uniquely formed, and, I would like to say, it gains its uniqueness through abstraction from the two large groups of culture, from 'objective' and from 'personal' culture.

And now to the question: What is the connection between the two major complexes of technology and culture described above? The connections are naturally twofold: they may be the effects that culture exercises on technology; or the effects that technology exercises on culture.

To consider the first, it is necessary to establish which possibilities lie within a specific culture or cultural realm to enable the development of technology;

and, on the other hand, which interests in that culture or cultural realm foster the development of technology. What I mean is this: a cultural realm might be part of institutional culture – the state, for example. The state creates certain developmental possibilities for technology. It can, for example, bring about conditions of peace, or pass a good patent law that will foster the development of technology. The next question is, then: in which cultural areas do the circumstances arise that enable technology to develop? They could arise in any area, but are naturally likely to be strongest in the economic area. A culture might arise in this area that encourages the development of a particular type of technology. Examples might be the foundation of organizations to foster, say, manual or hand-crafting skills (*Handwerk*), or the emergence of even larger forms of economic organization such as the capitalist system. From capitalist economic organization emerge much stronger interests or energies tied up with the development of technology than emerge from, say, organizations for manual or handicraft skills.

When considering the connections between technology and culture, what springs to mind is the second of the two types of connection mentioned above: the effects of technology on culture. I have stressed the first type: the effects of culture on technology, only because it completes the picture.

In order to characterize the effects of technology on culture, I advance the thesis that all areas of human culture, from the outermost extremes of material culture to the most personal culture, depend on primary culture. I would now like to clarify this with a few examples – I give a few examples because, obviously, I cannot offer an exhaustive analysis in a short lecture. I must be satisfied with hints; I must be satisfied with hints [*sic*] to show to you the possibilities.

I would like to mention at the outset: the proof for this thesis, for the correctness of this thesis, is given first in the empirical-historical way in which the examples are enumerated; and second, by deductive reasoning, that is, in a certain sense is a priori.

First: there is no cultural manifestation that is not based in some way on dependence on primary technology. Material culture is based on the existence of material goods, and these are simply the result of technology. Indeed, material culture is nothing more than a specific expression of the application of a specific technology. All the goods that we own and use are produced using certain procedures, which we know and are willing to use. No further explanation of this is therefore necessary.

Now, we move gradually from the outermost extreme where culture and technology in a sense overlap, to areas that – if I may be allowed to say – have always had less permanence and always contain less material.

First let us consider an aspect of institutional culture – the economy is, of course, the closest area to it to look at. That the economy depends on technology for its formation is scarcely disputable, even if the connections are not always uncovered in the best and most thorough way. To remind us of just a few closely connected facts. In order to develop, the organization to encourage the production of hand-crafted goods needs a lower level of development of production on the one hand, and a particular type of technology, namely empirical, on the other. By contrast, capitalism relies on a high level of production. Since capitalism rests on the separation of the classes, so that income is generated from work, production levels must be high enough to produce goods in quantities above and beyond that necessary to generate enough income for the workers to subsist.

Or let us take the development of the modern forms of wholesale trade (*Großhandelsformen*), or the modern retail trade. They are both directly connected to the development of the modern transport technology that first made these forms of economic organization possible. Today's trade organizations are built on them.

The size of a state depends on the measure of its transportation technology, and the intensity of its level of the interaction of its citizens depends on the extent of this measure. Let us compare a great state of antiquity with a modern great state, in which the degree of interaction – if I may be allowed to say it, the united-ness, of the population of the great modern state – rests simply on the transportation technology of our time. Or, to give another example from the area of state culture: The modern state grew out of the modern army, the modern army developed from the use of mercenaries, etc, and that is connected with the development of gunpowder. Thus, the entire development of the modern state depends on this fundamental discovery – just as the structure of society at its beginning was shown to rest on the development of war technology, weapons technology, methods of defence, etc.

However, it is impossible to consider the existence of a more remote area, such as the church, without thinking about some specific technological foundation. First: the fact that the personnel and other accoutrements of the church exist is due to the fact that production reached a certain level. The fact that certain 'servants of the church' [*Troß*, literally 'hangers-on'] could live and that certain groups [*Menge*, literally 'crowd'] of churches could be supported, presupposes the development of a particular form of technology.[1] For example, the evolution of the life of monks, of a monastery economy (*Klosterwirtschaft*)

---

1 Sombart's point is that these 'servants of the Church' are really sponging off others – thus, his use of *Troß* ('baggage', 'followers') and *Menge* ('crowd', 'mass', 'swarm', 'horde'; or a large number, a large amount).

during the Middle Ages belong here, in order to establish the connections. However, the development is also evident in another example of the domain of church culture – church pomp, the introduction of certain adornments, vestments, artistic tools and the like, is obviously linked to each different church activity, and presupposes a certain degree of technology, a specific form of possible technical formation (*Gestaltungsmöglichkeit*).

Let us then cast a glance at spiritual culture, which depends on the development of technology to the same extent.

Science! Science appears to take an entirely independent path of development, and yet if we look closer, certain minutiae (*Kleinigkeiten*), play an important role in scientific development. For example, I think of the reproduction or the restoration of a collection of prehistoric art, or I think of the possibility of publishing historical sources. Today, when we consider the history of science, is it to a large part grounded in specialist publications, which naturally lead to the conclusion that a certain amount of wealth (*Reichtumsgrad*) must have existed in the past. The degree of wealth presupposes the existence of certain technologies, particularly reproduction technologies. The production of paper is as cheaply as it is produced today, so that the printing press and its associated technology were founded on the basis of a limitless supply of paper.

The applications of natural science belong here, as indeed they depend on technology to a greater extent. The application of all apparatus and instruments is necessary for the accretion of natural scientific knowledge. For example, our astronomy is as dependent on the development of the telescope as is our biological research on the development of the microscope. All these made possible the first insights on which all further knowledge is built. The development of the knowledge and procedures of chemistry is the basis of the discoveries of medical science. I need not remind you of '606'[2] to show you that this is the closest connection between these two disciplines, for the developmental movement of technology and, for example, the procedures that encourage healing, are essentially a technical elaboration.

Medical science overlaps with its different neighbouring areas. I choose a branch: modern experimental psychology is essentially bound to technology

2 '606' was Salvarsan 606, the first 'magic bullet', discovered in 1909 by Paul Ehrlich, a German physician who later won the Nobel Prize for Medicine or Physiology. Ehrlich worked on staining tissues and found that dyes could be used to make certain bacteria visible. He realized that this could be used to send drugs directly to bacteria he wanted to kill without harming other parts of the body and found that an arsenic-based compound would kill syphilis spirochaete. Salvarsan 606 (named after the 606th drug in the sequence tested by the Ehrlich team) was heralded as a miracle cure soon after its commercial release, but became controversial when it was found to have severe side-effects and limited effectiveness in syphilis treatment. I wish to thank an LUP Editor for this information.

with its development; and its development is furthered by the possibility of the manufacture of finer measuring instruments, counting instruments, counting apparatus and the like. Modern philology is being built more and more on phonetic apparatus, on the possibility of measuring the oscillations and, with that, the pitch of the voice; and from those to the analysis of tone formation, letter formation (consonants, vowels), etc.

Art! If we consider the condition of our literature and pictorial art today, we will have an overall recurrent impression of an extraordinary abundance of production. In any case, production is a specialty of our contemporary artistic culture. Now production is naturally closely bound up with the development of technology, so it is necessary to break it down into its elements. If there are so many prolific writers today, and so many artists, too, the cause is, first and foremost, that our powers of production have reached a high level. Only when we have achieved a certain degree of wealth (*Reichtumsgrad*) can a greater number of men while away time in (if I am permitted to say the word) idleness (*Nichtstun*). In earlier times, almost everyone must have been engaged in manual production, even if an individual also wanted to be a minnesinger[3] (maybe a 'shoemaker and minnesinger') – if he were not in the fortunate position of being a landowner with tenant farmers, who would pay him, so that he could count on the income and thus be a minnesinger. This possibility, that a plethora (*Troß* – literally, in this sense, 'great clump') of, say, artistic works can result from production and thus a consequence of technology, is something we now also maintain in the widest sense of this connection. Here, I emphasize again for a moment how this consequence manifests itself in an unexpected way in the art of poetry.

Moreover, in the art of poetry, for example, the choice of motifs is connected to technology. Recently, an interesting enquiry was made into the presumption of death in poetry, and it led to the proof, which indeed lies close at hand, that all earlier poetry had made an extraordinarily extensive use of the presumption of death. In antiquity, for example, the *Oresteia* is only possible because Iphigenia cannot send any news home. Jocasta would have never married her son and the terrifying misery over Thebes would never have happened, if a connection had been established between Thebes and Corinth. In the *Twins* by Paulus, the two brothers who were separated from each other in early childhood would never have met each other accidentally as grown men in the same city. This would also be impossible today.

The same was true in the Middle Ages when we still had forests everywhere, in which a person could disappear. Where would Genofefa and Griseldis stay

---

3 *Minnesänger* – a medieval German term often applied to those religious 'poets' such as the thirteenth/fourteenth–century mystic, Heinrich Seuse.

today? They would have nowhere to go. The legends that once stemmed from the dead being found again among confusions and mistaken identities are predicated on the non-existence of our modern transport technology. Shakespeare also operated to a large extent with the same types of situations and, for example, based them on the extraordinary ignorance of geography of his times. It is interesting to observe how the region in which a person could disappear was always increasingly pushed to the periphery. For a time, America was that region, from which an unknown person could emerge or where a known person could disappear.

Even Tennyson in his *Enoch Arden* had to send his heroes to India. Today, the only equivalent region in which such an experiment could be made would be the North Pole, for even if someone disappears on an African expedition, a second one is dispatched to see what happened to the first. Thus, you see, ladies and gentlemen, how an apparently distant problem as the choice of poetic motifs is really closely connected with the problems of technology.

I will take another example to show where modern connections operate: modern music. The existence of modern music naturally presupposes the peculiarity of the producers and the consumers. First the consumers. It is necessary first to assume that they are there. But they are there only because of the milieu in which they have grown up. It is not far-fetched to connect the noise (*Lärm*) of modern music with the noise (*Lärm*) of the modern big city; in the same way as relaxing (*gelassene*) music is compared with the tranquility of a small town (*Kleinstadt*). An even closer connection must be made with the public audience. The deciding factor in the development of a particular cultural phenomenon (*Kulturerscheinung*) as modern music is that at the forefront is a public audience. Classical music was not written for the public as is today's music; classical music was produced for an intimate circle. Modern music is written *pour le monde* and this *monsieur tout le monde* is either raised in a big city or enabled, by the existence of modern transport, to arrive at a venue in order to hear a piece of music. Both genesis possibilities (*Entstehungs-Möglichkeiten*) are of technological nature, as seen in the big city and in the ease of transport.

The fact that today, so many women belong to the public is naturally also, in essence, a technological problem. The modern woman has emerged because the old household economy has collapsed, and she now has time to do more than just manage the economy, i.e. care for the house. As long as the woman managed the old household economy, the women's issue (*Frauenfrage*) was not a possibility, because there was no time and also no desire to develop one. In the evenings, a woman was so tired that she was happy when she could go to sleep. Thanks to the development of modern technology, this woman is thrown out of her household economic misery and now stands before the problem of

101

how to be occupied in some fashion, a problem that leads along many different paths, such as striving after careers, etc. One path leads to the frequenting of our lending libraries, concerts, etc.; but, this particular consumption of our modern art and literature is a natural outlet for the career-less or under-occupied woman [woman of leisure] of certain social strata.

If I want to bring modern music and technology into conjunction in another point – or, as one could say, into a certain relatedness, since from Richard Wagner and Richard Strauss, the appearance of new music paralleled the development of modern technology. The main enjoyment of Richard Strauss is when he uniquely integrates a new instrument into his symphony. If you compare the sound effect of Wagner's music and Strauss's music with the sound effect of Beethoven's music you will see clearly that here the essential difference is essentially a technical one. There are other wind instruments, but it is especially the development of the woodwind instruments that defines modern music.

Related to this aspect of scientific culture, artistic culture could perhaps be called *the* achievement of our age. It best exemplifies the wide expansion of the fabric of our culture. Similarly, mass production is a specialty of our time. Never before have building blocks of culture been used in such a way as to benefit the population with, for example, the network of sewers that has been developed today. This entire network of interconnections, if I may call it that, is, naturally, the result of the application of modern technology.

Earlier today we heard about the press and its significance. Now, the press is obviously a definitive cultural factor and it has become so through the development of the technology of production. For the modern press could not exist without an infinite supply of paper, the rotational printing press, or the telephone and telegraph. The interconnections of technology are evident in this field – but even more when the building blocks of culture cause expansion into, say, really cheap editions such as the Reclam volumes.[4] Indeed, how could a ten-pfennig little volume be produced without an infinite paper supply, cellulose-based paper, and the rotational printing press? Or, for example, how else could the arrangements for a series of lectures be made except on the basis of modern transport technology. Today, during the winter, there is no place in any cultured city that does not invite a university professor to visit, to, as it were, 'pour forth' (*verzapft*)[5] for its edification. Travel by post coach was

---

4 Sombart refers to the books that were made widely available through extraordinarily inexpensive editions. These were offered at a fraction of a cost of most other volumes.

5 'To dish out', 'to talk rot' – these are some possibilities for *verzapft*. I chose 'pour forth' because of its connection with the pouring forth of beer from the keg. Sombart is probably not excluding himself from this unflattering description.

obviously not as comfortable as is travel today. Only when it is possible to travel from Berlin to Königsberg in one night can a Berlin professor speak in the winter in Königsberg, Munich, etc.

Now it is also next to this formation of objective culture (cultural possession), that in the wide range of personal culture in all its emanations depends on technology. Indeed, it is based upon that and I feel extremely justified in saying that it seems to me that in general we must connect human worth with the use of tools. What is unique about human beings, the rationality of their activities, their goal-setting, is – as Noiré and others have described it – their fine-tuned development. The hand, with a tool or a weapon – which are both equally significant – developed so that even today the best definition of the species 'man' is Benjamin Franklin's expression: [man is a] 'tool-making animal'.[6] Even today, this use of technology determines more than personality, how the head and the soul are formed. You need only think about the effects that modern flight technology has on man – indeed, the effects that the automobile has on man. Compare a chauffeur with the driver of a horse-drawn carriage and you have before you two different human types, and their differences essentially lead back to their use of two different types of transport technology.

The influence of the environment on humanity can also be shown here. The din (*Lärm*), the haste, the fast speed of our lives, the tempo of our lives, the thousand impressions that the outside world offers us during our lives – these have an extraordinarily determining effect on the formation of the personality and are the immediate results of technology.

As these few examples have shown, there is a connection between technology and culture – technology can have a significant effect on culture. As I have said, the proof can be pursued in two ways. The second type of proof, the deductive, may be set out in few words, as follows. Every cultural act has a factual substrate, which may be used to produce some object. Every, or at least practically every [cultural act], belongs to the practice of a cultural act that enables man to live. If he is to live, he must have previously produced things. As he lives and acts, he must, in practically every circumstance, use things that have been produced. Even the hermit has his little house, the bell that he rings, and even his wretched little holy prayer book. These objects appear to force themselves on us for the completion of the cultural act. [They remain] 'an earthly burden to carry in embarrassment'. That is the meaning of all cultural activity. But, because that is so, it follows that the formation of this factual substrate, that objects necessary to cultural activity naturally work for the formation of the cultural act itself, [they] specifically work through quantity and number.

---

6 I have not located this maxim of Benjamin Franklin. Sombart gives it in English.

The outstanding significance that technology has for culture is thus indisputable. Its significance is so great that in some minds it has led to the acceptance (and with this I have reached the last of my arguments, namely, the question of the scientific utilization or treatment of the problem) that culture is an inevitable result of the appearance of technology, that culture is almost a function of technology. The classic expression of this concept is found in the so-called materialist conception of history. This materialist conception of history is a conclusion, a technological conception of history, if we accept Marx's informal descriptions of it. Finally, Marx's conditions of production could not be other than the technological conditions under which men operate economically. A clear, thoroughly thought-out formulation of the materialist conception of history would therefore set out in two propositions:

First proposition: The economy is a function of technology.

Second proposition: The remaining culture is a function of the economy.[7]

Now I consider it wrong that technology should be the principle on which the superstructure of the entire development of humanity is built. I believe that both parts of the above thesis cannot be maintained. First, economy is not a function of technology. It is assumed that with function there is a specific economic form that must correspond to a specific technology. That is incorrect, because a specific technology need not come into existence, even if knowledge of the procedure for bringing it into existence already exists. We must always distinguish between a latent technology and a technology that has come into existence. At any time, a procedure can be known but not carried out. If I want to describe economic life in general or all culture as a function of technology, I must prove that a potential technology necessarily leads to an actual technology. But, that is not the case. The application of a potential technology may not exist, or the application may be left unrealized intentionally or from indolence. For example, an entire population can resolve not to use an existing technology. There is no reason why a culture should be forced to use technology to do anything. It is entirely possible that in the future, all modern methods of transport will not be used, although they are all possible. It is said – although we have no information about it – that culture in China had developed to the point where the Chinese achieved various technological breakthroughs and resolved not to concern themselves further with 'this rubbish' (*Kram*), since it is irrelevant to this life. This is the same as not applying existing technology because of indolence, and that happens every day. If I wanted to prove that the

7 Sombart writes *übrigen Kultur* so I have rendered this as 'remaining culture' but it seems to me that his claim concerns culture in general. I think this because he seems to think that Marx believes that economy = technology = culture. Whether Sombart is correct in this I cannot say; but he was certainly very familiar with Marx's writings.

economy is a function of technology, and, *nota bene*, I wanted to prove this a priori, it is the presupposition of the materialist conception of history in its original sense that I would use. I could never explain why modern technology is not used in certain contemporary economies; for if I wanted to add: 'because no economic pressure is present', I would introduce an entirely different factor into the proof.

Second, even if we also consider the application of technology, we find that there is no conclusive evidence that a certain technology need be applied in any specified economy. We observe more often that, on the contrary, an economy rests on various different technological bases; and that the same technology is used in different economies. An economic system may have different techno-logical foundations. For example, capitalism can rest on empiricism; rationalism can rest on hand technology or machine technology. On the other hand, a particular technology can belong to entirely different economies. Machines may be used equally successfully in capitalist and socialist economies. If I really wanted conclusive evidence of the functioning of an economy, alternatives would and must be excluded.

But, now even if we also want to assume that the economy is a function of technology, the proof naturally still leads more or less to the claim that the remaining culture is a function of the economy – or the claim fails to be proved for two reasons: first, because the proof cannot lead to the claim that the remaining culture is a function of the economy; and second, it is possible to observe that the claim cannot be true, because technology usually works directly, rather than through the medium of the economy. When I said a short while ago that the emergence of modern music depended on the development of instrument technology, no economic factor is included in this effect. This is a direct effect of technology on an extra-economic cultural act.

Why it cannot be proved that culture is a function of technology, meaning the economy, is evident from a look at how technology works. We must again differentiate between the introduction of a technique and the effects of an introduced technique. The introduction of a technique is a possibility, as I have just demonstrated, not a necessity; a possibility that can be put into effect for many different reasons. When a technique is introduced, it realizes a techno-logical possibility. Then we can and rightfully should present the effect of this technological achievement as a condition for the execution of certain cultural acts. From there we must look beyond speaking of it as a *causa causans*, as a particularly effective cause, since in the face of all natural happenings we must postulate as living human beings. To the living human being who wishes to execute some cultural act, technology will approach it as an objective condition, under which this cultural act can and will execute some motivating cultural act.

I would like to place technology in the cultural picture, since technology can have extraordinarily diverse effects. Here, too, I can offer to give just a few examples, if I am permitted, because the time I was allowed is moving along.

Technology can have direct and indirect effects. Its effect is direct when a cultural area is directly influenced; it is indirect when a cultural area is affected by other cultural areas. Accordingly, 'personal' culture can be directly influenced by the use of a particular technology, for example, when I steer a car instead of a horse-drawn cab, or when I sit on a steam tractor rather than walk behind a horse-drawn plough.

From the points where the direct effect is present, the effect can obviously be transferred to other cultural areas – to state culture, for example: one state is like another if it is put together by other, similar individuals. The state can encroach on the economy and the state can encroach on 'personal culture', or on artistic and other types of culture, directly or indirectly. Influences naturally have an extraordinary range of possibilities.

Second, the effect can be active or passive, as I term it. Technology is active when it functions when I use it; it is passive when I suffer from it.[8] The effect of technology is equal, that I, when I – with the same example again – use a certain instrument to experience a particular formation of personality. The effect of technology is also, when I become nervous because of the eternal noise of the electric [trams] and the noise of cars and with the ringing of the telephone. In the first case it is active and in the second case it is a passive effect.

Third, the effect can be mediate or immediate.[9] The effect of technology is mediate when it is effected through its products, which are delivered finished. It may be effected through the mass of products, or through the type of production. Technology works in all cases through the mass of products, as I have shown, where the existence of a population or a class is made possible because production has been developed in a specific way. Technology is mediate in its effect when, for example, a particular instrument is used in its production – say, one of the instruments in the modern orchestra of instruments. By contrast, the effects are immediate when they follow the application of a particular technique. (Naturally, the effects of technology do not occur in parallel but in isolation.) One example is the effect that technology has on a worker, on the workplace, on the worker's health, on his psyche, etc. Here, the application works directly on the worker.

Finally, it is necessary to distinguish between a positive and a negative effect. Technology can work because it is there, and it can work because it is not there. We could clarify this for ourselves if we considered a whole series of

8 Sombart utilizes the distinction between active and passive, doing and being done to.
9 Sombart's distinction is between indirect and direct effects.

cultural manifestations emanating from the fact that a specific technology was not available. The crusades were plausible because that was a time in which there was no telephone. The combining of two such things is excluded.

Now gentlemen, it has been getting increasingly dark around us, but I hope not in your heads as well.

What final results can be drawn from these observations for scientific research? I will formulate them briefly as I see them:

First: that all cultural manifestations should be observed from the viewpoint of their technological establishment, so that anything approaching a technological–historical view would be rejected, as I have already described.

Second: that the universal dependence of all cultural manifestations specifically on the influences of technology, and the reflection of the influence of technology in every minor aspect of cultural science, should be opposed. Naturally, economic history has more to do with technology than the history of religion or the history of literature, but the history of literature would be eternally incomplete if the influence of technology was entirely left out of account.

Third: Different approaches must be brought to the treatment of the problem, the type of effect is fundamentally different. Research methods must be fundamentally different to establish the effects of technology on culture – so different approaches must be applied to the treatment of the problem. In a few cases, for example, the experimental methods used in biology, where something can be established through the sampling of specific influences on the body or on the mind, are most appropriate. In other cases, the comparative results method is the only one that will enable goals to be achieved.

Fourth: As an outcome for scientific research, another final result is to establish that the influences of technology must be considered in isolation from other influences. A bad mistake, frequently made today, is that technological influences are not considered apart from economic influences, for example. If I want to establish the effect of the machine on the worker, I must differentiate between the influences of technology and those of the economy – the effect of the machine in the capitalist economy is different from its effect in the socialist economy or on the everyday economy of the street. If I want to explain the effects of technology, I must naturally consider the economic mixture.

That was approximately, ladies and gentlemen, what I wanted to submit to you.

Perhaps for many of you I have not covered what you expected. I have said nothing regarding the cultural value of technology – and naturally, I fully intended to exclude it. The problem of the value of technology for humanity is without doubt that it should be considered partly as scientific. For example, it is possible to show that a number of so-called technological accomplishments that our age boasts about are no more than the wretched help necessary to remedy the bad conditions created by our culture in the first place. When I am proud that a big city has a good and brilliant transport network that can bring me quickly from the outskirts into the centre, it must be clear to me that this achievement first became necessary because the development of modern human culture forced people away from the centre of their activity. If I take great pride in our streets being lit, compared with centuries ago, when they were not, I must also make it clear to myself that street lighting has become necessary only because so many men walk around at night. If no one goes into the streets at night, there is no need to light the streets. There are thousands of examples to show that the so-called progress of technology is only a remedy for bad conditions that had not existed previously. A complete sewerage system is a remedy for the bad conditions created when men are forced to live crammed together in a huddle. It is therefore possible to shine scientific light on the problem of value. It is also possible to establish that there is a connection between individual cultural appearances and which values are destroyed and which are won. I have excluded this problem.

In the end, the question of cultural value is, like all values, a highly personal matter with which scientific knowledge has no concern. It is to be accepted as self-evident that each individual is conscious that the value of technological accomplishments must first be questioned, and that no one adopts the stand-point of the modern engineer and is enchanted by every technological innovation. Today, we do not simply recognize that a mere technological development is of cultural value. We are aware that we should ask critically: 'Is it really of value that we can fly around in the air or not?' I say that the decision of the value of a specific technology is in the highest degree a personal matter. There is no objective gauge to establish whether the Versailles castle is more valuable, as it was so beautifully described to us yesterday, with the etiquette of certain people, without any modern comfort, or an American tower block hotel or a modern Berlin apartment 'with all modern comforts', as its description reads. There is no objective gauge to determine whether one or the other is more valuable.

In any case, regarding the question of the cultural value of technology, there can be no doubt that that is a problem in itself, and should there be a discussion, I suggest to you that we leave this problem alone. I would like to ask you not to venture into this really tempestuous sea of cultural valuation; but rather ask you pleasantly to remain in the peaceful navigable waters that I have sailed us into and let us occupy ourselves with the explanation of the problems of an 'objective' causal connection between technology and culture.

(Applause.)

ERNST TROELTSCH

Stoic-Christian Natural Law and Modern Profane Natural Law[1]

[Friday Afternoon, October 21 1910
Opening Address by the chairman, Professor Simmel

Ladies and gentleman, I open this session and announce that, counting on your friendly agreement, the Executive Board has resolved that in our scientific assembly we will refrain for the foreseeable future from expressions of applause. Indeed, we are a very new Society and we are still fortunate in not having any ruinous castles or other landmarks in our past, so that we can make our own traditions instead of having to follow traditions from the past. Thus, we want to establish this tradition, since it also adheres to the principle of our Society that we should refrain from making value judgements. So, where possible, we want to lead by good example.

Now I give the floor to Professor Troeltsch – Heidelberg.]

It is not easy to agree about the task and the essence of sociology, but knowing how to ask questions in sociology and how to observe are obviously important, especially in view of the pressing need for historical research. Learning the right approach makes it possible to envisage the subject being investigated in different ways.

The following arguments are not intended to be instrumental in solving the great problems of sociology. They are intended merely to demonstrate the enlightening effects that questions formulated along sociological principles can

---

1 Troeltsch's paper is reproduced in Troeltsch, 1925: 166–191, with four important differences: 1) Troeltsch's first paragraph from the speech is omitted; 2) many sentences are omitted in the last several pages; 3) the discussion is not included; and 4) Troeltsch adds a footnote in which he advises the reader to refer to the *Soziallehren* for the details and the foundations of the paper. Troeltsch, 1925: 166.

have on a particular historical subject. In relation to the generally large themes of this Conference, this paper is only a very modest contribution, but it can show how it is possible to draw something useful from a still very incomplete science.

From the beginning, sociological investigation must make a fundamental distinction between sociological natural laws and the laws that might ideally be made by those who have power over ideas. To the first domain belongs knowledge, as in the circumstances of the extent of a sociological circle to the manner of the bonds of its members. The smallness of the circle corresponds to the personal and inward-looking immediacy of the ties, together with the danger of personal quarrels and separations. The largeness of the circle corresponds to the abstract and impersonal nature of the relationships, allied to the powerful and formal nature of the ties, together with the danger of the uniformity and powerlessness of the members. That is a socio-psychological natural law, one among countless others that may be regarded as marks of society and culture. To the second domain belong the ideal laws – the moralistic, the political, legal and religious laws that are formulated, and from which the psyche generates constellations and oppositions to master, to dominate, to make subservient, or to strive to overcome. The legal idea of property can be construed at the same time as juridical, as can the most varied ideal systems, including being considered in relation to the idea of immortality. This can be connected with the concept's own self-supporting significance, as a result of a natural economic process or facing another concept where it is sought fit to regulate and to master it. Conceptual fundamental ideal presentations and pure logical consequences are always at work here at the same time.

Laws of both types – the natural and the ideal – in their thousand-fold interconnections and interweavings determine the progressions of culture. To understand these, it is always essential to bear in mind the diverse origins and combinations of the opposing types of law and to analyse them with reference to movements and change. There is no history of culture that concentrates on the history of the development of the natural law of society; there is also no history that concentrates on development and the dialectic of ideas. All historical understanding shows the association and the opposition of both. Sometimes, the ideal legislations are wrecked on the natural laws of society or forced by them into the most complicated compromises. Sometimes they are able to improve, order, multiply and harmonize the movement of natural law and to make it serviceable. However, the opposition often also leads to a complete doubting of the world, to a quietist pessimism, or to a mystical indifference.

The attempt to unify these opposites or to dissolve them in a higher third can be forgotten about. They are always philosophical and in every case logical postulates, but they offer nothing for the historical understanding of the facts themselves. In particular, the economic theory of history, with its attempt to make ideal legislation a mirror image, and the sociological natural laws on which it is dependent, rest upon highly questionable speculation. Certainly and as a matter of course there exist connections here, but in the first place, the connection is reciprocal: as the sociological foundation determines the formation of ideas, so, conversely, does ideology intervene in the factual connections. Moreover, the connection signifies not simply mirror image and dependence: if the idea, the ethical, artistic, religious idea, reacts in a particular way, this reaction is not something that is built into the foundation of the idea. That reaction must in every case be investigated and the entire network of relations determined. Finally, where the ideal legislation also develops in connection with sociological natural foundations, it always contains so much that is unique; and a surplus results from one's own power, so that it at least leads to a relative independence and with that to one's own initiative on the influenced life in the environment. Any given formed ideas can only really and fundamentally be understood from history and from insight into their inner consequences. Only through the representation by the sociological natural law can the circumstances of the sharply differing opposition that occurs between the goals of the ideal legislation and the conditions of life, which are rarely completely extinguishable, be understood.

The religious idea of Christianity offers for our entire culture one generally important example of the opposition, completion, compromise and sacrifice from which arises the social ideal.

It is easy and simple to determine the social ideal, since, fundamentally, it emerges from the religious idea of Christianity. It is the idea of radical religious individualism submitting with moral obedience to the will of God, and through which the individual is metaphysically anchored with an indestructible faith. With the individual's acceptance of the will of God, however, an excessive elevation of the individual does not take place. Rather, all individuals meet in God and find themselves, and in this supra-human medium, all the common human oppositions – competition, selfishness and self-assuredness – are extinguished and transformed into reciprocal relations of love founded upon the will of God. Just as Jesus is God's idea to the Israelites, so we understand him as a living and creating will of God and with him, the unification of souls in one people or in the realm of God itself. A supra-worldly realm of love that is founded on souls built out from God is, therefore, the correlation of the idea of Jesus, and not a quietist mysticism. This love should make all law, power, and force unnecessary and should ground all mutuality on a personal conviction of solidarity. And, with that, all the common oppositions and superficialities will be overcome. In particular, it should also free the soul from the urge to possess and the thirst for pleasure and, instead, will incline itself towards modesty and frugality so as to harmonize into an unconditional mutual readiness to help and to communicate. The strongest opposition of this ideal to all the habits and demands of the world is sensed in Jesus' pronouncement. Therefore, he thinks of a complete realization first by erecting a new world order, when the heavenly Father in the fullness of his miraculous power leads up to the time of the complete and victorious dominance of the holy will in God's realm. Until then, his believers will collect themselves in stillness into the hoped-for community of the realm of God, and will prepare themselves externally, insofar as it is possible to be ready, to fulfil the will of God.

A new religious community was formed from this fundamental pronounce-ment, through the cult of Christ with the veneration of God embodied in Christ, and set itself apart from other religious communities; and, above all, this, with its purely religious-cultic connection, was a new sociological form. From the outset, this new form carried in itself a specific sociological ideal for its conception and formation, that ideal of the unification of a radical religious individualism with an equally radical religious socialism. However, it could not naturally overlook that this ideal could also have radiated into relations and concerns of the non-religious, profane life, that from there this ideal could also have been created. However, there was an immediate conflict present, not merely because of the different surroundings of the society of late antiquity but as a result of the many sociological natural laws and the demands of social life. The task was to comprehend and to overcome this opposition.

From the outset there are *three main types* involved in the solution of this task, which become even more strongly accentuated and contrasted in later history. They hang entirely together with the different points of departure of the sociological self-formation of the Christian-religious idea itself, and can only in their essence be grasped from there.

The most important and central sociological self-formation of the Christian idea is that of the *Church*. The essence of the Church type is observed as religious salvation, as something with the heavenly holy institution of the given, and principally as that which is already realized. Independent of the subjective performance and completeness, all salvation rests on the religious community through a finished and executed redemption arising from a bequeathed grace. It is grasped as an already provided salvation without the need for personal justice and works of grace. In grasping it lies the renunciation of one's self, and the single-willed, complete conviction that all else emerges out of inner necessity from one's self. Therefore, emerging from the funda-mental notion of grace, all that which is needed for complete salvation comes only from faith and through the death of Christ. However, for this objective salvation it demands the independent objectification of the subject through transformation and incarnation. That comes through the Church, which was founded by Christ and the Apostles and their priestly successors, who ministered to the living with thoroughly powerful sacraments given by him. From this idea, along with the growing strength of the objective foundation, arises Catholicism, with its dogma of redemption through God-men and with the investiture of this redemption in the Church's institution of salvation and grace. This churchly idea progressed, despite all the simplification of dogma, despite all elimination of the re-emerging strict emphasis on one's perform-ances and works; and despite all the emphasis on personal individual certainty from Protestantism of both main confessionals.[2] For the individual, the Christian institution of salvation and grace through the Church, which was received from Christ, mediates individual salvation purely on the foundation of submission to this objective whole. One does not offer any contributing significance of one's own performance to Christian-ethical perfection; salvation comes only through the imperfect result from the conviction of an emanating practice.[3] Salvation rests upon submission to the objective institution of grace and the office of the preacher.

The non-conquerable defects resulting from this submission to the emanat-ing practice stems from the never fully annulled sins, which, since the time of Adam have dominated all men and, only as a curse but never as a reality can they be completely cancelled. Through this entire inner structure comes the idea that the Church is capable of the renunciation of strict Christian perfection and compromise with the actual orders of the world and society in their sinful conditions. The Church also recognizes the sub-Christian (*unterchristlicher*), and the need for useful social and ethical orders for temporal discipline and order of the sinful world.

Sharply differentiated from this is the second self-formation of the Christian-sociological idea – the *sect type*. This type is rigorist; without compromise it will fulfil the demands of the evangelical ethic, especially the Sermon on the Mount. It does not capitulate before universal sinfulness and it does not take up the idea of a completed salvation and an already laid-out grace. Moreover, it craves a real overcoming of sins, the real observance of God's commands, and believes in total salvation only for those whose grace is given by the

---

2 By both main Protestant confessionals Troeltsch means Lutheranism and Calvinism. See Chapter 3, Sections 2 and 3 of *Soziallehren,* and 'Calvinismus und Luthertum – Überblick' ('Calvinism and Lutherism – An Overview'). In Troeltsch, 1925: 254–61.

3 Troeltsch does not mean 'practice' in the sense of repetition, but in the sense of an 'office'.

recognizable power of the Christian way of living. To the adherents of the sect, the community of religious life is not a universal, people-encompassing institution into which one is born, and the power of grace will be brought about by the influence of the Church, the priesthood and the sacraments. The adherent of the sect wants a holy community that emerges from an assembly of mature and conscious Christian peoples. Sermons, sacraments and the institutional community possess the means of assembly and care, but are not independent from the miraculous power of the subject and his own performance. He rejects the priesthood and affirms lay religion. Insofar as he accepts priests who produce holy results, it is because these stem from a faith in the personal holy individual power of their personalities, not in the power of their office. The sacraments are to him not the means of transmission of some fundamental capital foundation, but the devotions and confirmations from where springs the conscious will of the state of sanctification. In this sense, sects are found in the original Christian movement, from which the Church type had not yet clearly separated, and the Church was not yet a people's or an institutional church. The later sect clearly emerged with Monism and Donatism, continued into the Middle Ages in the Walderners and related groups, and has continued from the sects of the Reformation to today in countless new forms.[4] Catholicism had absorbed one part of the motive for sect-formation into the Church, as the monks' essence was part of the sects' ideal. The Franciscans, in particular, were originally a branch of the sect type; later, with their powerful church melding, they lost their original character. Luther, too, with his analyses of the Sermon on the Mount, also counts as a member of the sect type.

The essence of today's sects and religious communities brings them to a position below the surface, but as a not insignificant power in the complete contemporary society. It stands to reason that from the beginning, this sect type must scorn the churches of the people, and the institutional Church, that his impetus is to replace the institutional character of the church with the voluntary community of the sect, and, above all, he shuns and rejects any compromise with the culture and education of profane society and its sub-

---

4 They are all Christian sects. Monism was begun by the Phrygian prophet in the second century. Donatism was a rigorous North African sect that began to flourish in the fourth century. The Walderners were found in the border regions between Italy and France, beginning in the thirteenth century. In 1910 several thousand were living in places as diverse as Europe and South America, and several hundred in New York. For this and other footnotes I have consulted *Die Religion in Geschichte und Gegenwart (Religion in History and the Present)*, Tübingen, 1908–1913. This massive five-volume work was the combined effort of the most learned German theologians of the time. Troeltsch himself contributed more than a handful of articles. While the third and now the fourth edition of this work are helpful, I have relied on the first edition.

Christian standards for life. He will be as hostile to compromise and culture as the Church is friendly to both. His strict Christian radicalism generally collides hard with sociological natural law and social ideals, and in these collisions are its peculiar social particularities and effects expressed.

A third type is *enthusiasm*[5] and *mysticism*. Mysticism stresses the immediacy, the presence and the inward focus of the religious experience, the need to jump clear of traditions, cults and institutions, or the complete, immediate exchange with the spiritual authorities. The mysticism type sees the historical and the institutional as mere stimulations and a means of release for the immediate inner communication with God. In this sense, mysticism expressed itself early on in the original Christian enthusiasm, in the doctrine of possession of the secrets of the Godhead and in the immediate revealing or completing and continuing spirit. The religiosity of St Paul is especially permeated with such mysticism, which, however, is held in a state of deep inner tension with his ideas of redemption, salvation and institution. Christian mysticism was fully strengthened through the acceptance of Neo-Platonic mysticism. Its result remains in a process of emanation of finite spirits from God, and God's latent presence is in these spirits. A seed or a spark of God's being leads through the thinking and sinks into the secrets of the essential base of the soul, and again leads upwards, back to substantial unity with the godly essence. These thoughts in each case grasped the objectivity of the cults and the dogma of the institutions, with their unsatisfactory inward-directed feeling, which, once awakened, lived in an inner movement of life in the revelation and presence of God.

Mysticism in the more enthusiastic–pneumatic sense, or in the more Pauline sense of history and letters, through the overwhelming sense of the inner combination with the timeless Christ principle, or, finally, in a pantheistic, Neo-Platonic sense, permeates the entire history of Christianity. Mysticism remains more Christian the more it emphasizes the personal quality of God and the purpose of human life. It distances itself from the mass of Christianity to the extent that it lets itself merge into the Neo-Platonic conception of God as a resting on an absolute Being without predicates, and lets the mystic submerge into God. Yet, it is only in mysticism that the truth of the immediacy of the community of God is found. Therefore, its externalities are fundamentally different from those of the spirit of the sects, which adhere exactly to the historical letters and the historical sermons and the organization of the holy community. Mystics agree with the sect only in the position of indifferences to the world or hostilities to the world. They agree that the spirit of God lies far

5 Troeltsch is using 'enthusiasm' in its German religious context, meaning highly non-rational, hence mystical.

above sensibility, the world and the finite, and gladly use this idea to express the demands of the Sermon on the Mount as an expression of the overcoming and setting aside of natural self-affirmation. However, it is also understood differently here; not as the rigour of spirituality, but as the mortification of the natural drives of the flesh and the release of the supra-sensible submission of the spirit to the Spirit. It can occur in the ascetic form as well as in the libertine, both of which occur in the expressed forms and show indifference to the world. Even here, the sociological consequences are entirely different from those of the sect.

In truth, mysticism is a radical individualism, independent of community. Independent of history, cults, and external mediation, the Christian mystic stands in direct communication with Christ or with God. In this direct communication, the practical results of submission collect themselves as a process to a supra-sensible life beyond. Social relations exist only in the natural binding of the individual, like-minded souls, who are bound together in their inner process and in the communality of understanding. No cultural community, no organization needs to emerge here. Insofar as the fundamental content of their life is mystical, hermits and monks have a small circle of friends of God, which is expressed in the stillness of the land of brotherly love. It is in this sociological form that mysticism of this kind expresses itself. This is bound up with an unlimited tolerance, which is effectively seen as the core of all religious processes. From their external life comes a forced community that makes a ruin of the inward-looking, personal life. Relationships with the profane world are disdained, with the exception of the universal conviction of love, from which all meet together in the inner life of God. Only that is accepted which can utilize the overcoming of self-satisfaction and leads essentially to indifference and restraint towards all worldly forms of life and life interests that cannot be united with the mystical life in God. Those relations belong to the world and to the flesh that either one tolerates without inner involvement, as long as his time continues or the mystic and his circle of friends disavow.

From each of the three main types described, it is now necessary to discuss and explain the differences between natural necessities and the non-Christian ideals of social life. The most important in universal-historical terms is the Church. It has the strongest powers to disseminate, diffuse and organize. With the state and society, it completes life. It accepts worldly culture and civilization within its possible limits. However, it also represents a particularly strong religious idea that maintains grace and freedom independently of the mass of religious compulsion of the Christian demand for Christian morality in God's trust and in the salvation that transcends the world.

The question here is first and foremost: How has the Church evolved its relationship to non-Christian facts and ideals of social life, and with what inner thoughtful motivation could it develop them?

The short answer to this question is: it did this through the development of the concept of Christian natural law and through the conquest of all those elements with the aid of this natural law.

Word and deed clamour for an explanation. Natural law, or more specifically the concept of an ethical natural law out of which all legal and social rules and institutions emerge, is a creation of the Stoa. The Church derived this concept from general intuition (*Anschauung*) in a world ruled by law and, from the application of the world law, drew up the ethical and legal rules for self-affirmation and exemplification of spirit. Having achieved this, it increasingly left its pantheistic foundations behind, and described ethical natural law since Poseidonois and then especially during the Roman Stoa in terms of an almost theistic sense of an expression of the holy will.[6] There is also a countermovement in the direction of the Judaeo-Christian idea that all humans are bound together with the emanating ethos from the will of God. Still more important, however, is the reference of the law.

The Stoic legal and social philosophy is, like the entire Stoic ethic, a product of the disintegration of the ancient *polis* and the world-kingdom of a created cosmopolitan horizon. In place of positive law and morality emerges the ethic derived from a universal, law-abiding reason. In place of the national interests of his native country (*Heimat*), the individual is fulfilled by God's reason; in place of the single political connection is the idea of humanity that lacks differentiation in terms of state and place, race and colour. From this human ideal comes a fully free *Gemeinschaft* or community. It obeys God's laws of reason and is separate from the drives (*Treibleben*) of independent men.[7] It is at the same time without force, without social power and class differences, and without these differences [the members] lack private property and are bound together in a freer human community of respect and love (*Achtungs- und Liebesgemeinschaft*). In this *Gemeinschaft*, only the dominance of all members is expressed through holy natural law.

However, the Stoa could not hide that this is an ideal state (*Idealstand*), which cannot be realized, given world conditions. From this, the Stoa differentiated between an absolute natural law and a relative natural law. The first was real only in the golden age of humanity, either in the early, seminal state or in the full representation of the ideal. However, under the conditions of intruding human passions, the seeking of dominance and avarice, individual

6 Poseidonos was an Ancient Athenian politician.
7 By 'independent' Troeltsch does not mean *political* independence. Rather, he speaks of the separate individuals in contrast to the common members of the *Gemeinschaft*.

will and aggression, the full realization of [the absolute natural law] was not possible. Under these practical conditions, ethical reason was forced to find a means of guaranteeing the possibility of the ideal. This occurred through the development of a systematic political power, of property, of natural laws guaranteeing justice, marriage and the family order, and of a sanctioned regulation of inequality. Through reason, without carrying a non-predictive particular account of the possibility of the ideal, natural law is made possible by positive law in light of the present limitations governed by the conditions prevailing in the world. Universal human right exists through a rationally produced compromise between positive law and the law of reason, although its rational working out is obviously still demanded. As is known, these thoughts emerge from Roman into Byzantine law.

The Stoa had already scientifically and dialectically worked through a problem that was also put to the ethics of Christians. Both, Stoicism and Christianity were entwined many times at the root, as a result of the turning inwards, the individualizing and simultaneous universalizing that came with the religious idea as regeneration out of a disempowered world, from the collapse of the state ethics and folk morality (*Volkssitte*) of antiquity. It is therefore natural that the Christians borrowed from the Stoa the results of the efforts they had devoted to related problems, despite the many differences between them. Christians identified the Christian ideal of freedom of God's children and the community of unconditional love (*Liebesgemeinschaft*) with the Stoic absolute natural law. And just as the Stoics believed that its realization occurred only in the golden age of primeval humanity, so did the Christians believe that it was fully realized in the paradise of the protoplasm. The Stoic dominance of reason over the life of passion (*Triebleben*) and the Stoic doctrine of a human community of equal and free persons in holy law appeared in fact to be identical to Christian holiness and Christian love.

But Christians could also incorporate a doctrine of relative natural law. As the Stoics taught that the seeking of domination, of selfishness and avarice destroyed the original harmony, equality and freedom, the Christians were aware from the Bible that corruption was the original blasphemy of humanity that led back to them. From the condition of sin sprang the need to work, and with that went property, and from it also sprang marriage and the family order of rules of governing newly awakened sexual passion. From Cain's crime came the legal and retributional orders. Nimrod's founding of the state was the beginning of law, power and the force of the princes. The splitting of the people with the destruction of the tower of Babylon was the disintegration of humanity into nations. Cham's blasphemy produced slavery, and on that rests a great part of the economic order. However, as the reason of the Stoa created new societal orders for discipline, order and ethics, and blasphemy against God, the results of sin were transformed into ways of imposing penalties and ways of attaining salvation from sins. These serve the regulation and disciplining, the punishment and the struggle against sins, as the populace (*bürgerliche*) and economic order as the presuppositions of an inner and personal ethic (*Sittlichkeit*).[8]

Of course, Christianity does not abandon the absolute natural law as fully as the Stoa. It is maintained in its identification with the master command of the Sermon on the Mount for special and true Christians, as against the Christian masses and the average Christian. It carries on in Christian morality as that famous and deep-seated difference between strict Christianity in the sense of the Sermon on the Mount, but does not appear as the unconditional duty for all – rather as a suggestion, advice for dealing with the conditions of life and an individual assessment of how to realize the complete Christian ideal of the qualified and the called. The reduction of Christianity for the masses in the relative order and activity of natural law and in relation to strict Christianity can be realized only so far as is possible under these conditions. It is a compromise of strict Christianity with the demands of active life, and a relative assessment of the ethical and legal institutions of non-Christian and pre-Christian circles of life in regard to the question of whether personal subjective performance of holiness of such gradation was possible. Such a compromise was possible only in the Church, because the sacred is not bound to the strengths of personal performance, but to the objective means of help for the transmission of institutional grace. In this aspect, both classes of Christians are again equal. The unity was one of the main issues and guaranteed, and only in those marginal issues, even if they were important, was such a moderation possible for the masses regarding the question of personal subjective performance of holiness. It is clear how closely connected the concept of such a relative natural law is with the Church and its objective holiness, by contrast with the subjective performance of an independent power of salvation.

That is how the concept of Christian natural law and its infinite richness of consequences developed. It is, however, important to now explain this double-edged concept and to show how its contradictions stemmed from its origin and affected its later historical development. For this relative natural law, specifically its relativity, it can be emphasized that it is a consequence of sins and the need to penalize sins. Then, as it did to St Augustine, the state, law, property, the entire culture in general, appears to be the work of sin. As a result of the conflict in the Gregorian Church, it can be shown that the Church introduced

8 Troeltsch uses the common term *Burger* to mean a member of a political or civic community. Here he means 'political' by contrast with 'economic'.

its deeply subordinated institution for the punishment of sins (*Sündenstiftung*). Furthermore, the need for discipline and order for all was emphasized. Churchly natural law appeared to be the glorification of authority, with humble submission under force only through patriarchy, with a milder subordination to the ruling powers in the areas of the state, the family, vassals and bondage. In connection with that, it appears as holy punishment and holy intervention in history and it is often received as an entirely positive expression of an arbitrary (*willkürliche*) holy act.[9] Conversely, the naturalness and the reasonableness of natural law again can be placed in the forefront. For it appears as the outflow of natural light, of reason, of the order of creation, and as the rational foundation of the Church and the ethics of grace (*Gnadensittlichkeit*). Then, it is simply constructed from reason, and must be valid even if God did not exist. Thus, a rational doctrine of state, society, legal and economic rule is developed, which is most possibly connected to the social philosophy of antiquity. The entire area of profane life is independently regulated and rejected only where the Church justified intervention in holy positive law and made it necessary. In the same measure, the democratic, equal, liberal, socialistic strains of natural law can come forth. Churchly natural law can proclaim the revolution against the godless princes and possibly also proclaim tyrannicide. It can represent the peoples' sovereignty (*Volkssouveränität*) and a Christian socialism up to the boundary of communism. Gregory VII cursed the political creation of natural law as a creation of sins to honour the Church, yet simultaneously prescribed Christian democracy and the peoples' sovereignty against the godless as a reasonable goal of failing authority.

All aspects of Christian natural law were not yet present in the early, pre-medieval Church. Here, world culture and Christian rigorism were still basically split. Monks were the valve through which this tension was discharged. In the medieval Church and culture, in which the religious and the profane, the churchly and the wordly grew together into a great living unity, and as the monks became more like the Church's bodyguards, the concept of natural law displayed its full significance. From St Thomas there was created a scientific (*wissenschaftliche*) form that continues until today and is always repeated anew in the infinite Catholic literature on state law (*Staatsrechtsliteratur*). The essence of this churchly cultural morality is the pathway from nature to grace. *Gratia praesupponit ac perficit naturam*[10] is the phrase. Is it possible to develop the natural order of relative natural law as the foundation of the entire churchly culture? The historical process in which the legal order has been formed can be viewed as an indirect manifestation of the working out of the holy institution

9 See page 71 note 7 for clarification of this term.
10 'Grace presupposes a perfect nature.'

through the natural course of things. All the creations of positive law will therefore become sacred and they will initially be respected as *poena et remedium peccati*.[11] Will sins of certain magnitudes and those with the local circumstances of specific specialities of pure, positive human law be brought closer to the rational and the absolute, and their contradictory forms of life (*Lebensformen*) be kept away, at least in theory? The mood of submission to the prevailing powers and orders and the submission to the inequalities, to the recognition of slavery and bondage, the patriarchal feeling of obedience and the duty of solicitude (*Fürsorgepflicht*) – all appear as the content of natural law. But this same natural law transforms itself into the highest revolutionary and radical principle against all powers, laws and orders. The reasonable goal of such support of discipline, order and harmony can no longer be fulfilled, or at least even difficulties are readied for the holy effects of the kingdom of grace (*Gnadenreiche*), the Church. Here, then, the substitution of laws enacted contrary to reason (*vernunftwidrigen Rechtes*) by something reasonable is permitted – indeed, even demanded. The arbitrariness (*Willkür*) and the anarchy of such criticisms of reason are only prevented by the fact that ultimately it is the Church that can decide the right (*Recht*) of resistance and of the new order. The Christianity of the newly formed justice of criticism or of revolution is, however, determined entirely through the goals of reason and is always developed only with regard to the conditions of the state of sin and the leading power of the Church. In this sense, natural law or natural right is understood as all-powerful and as the greatest lever of cultural progress, as Catholicism understands it even today. Considering this, even today it proclaims itself at the greatest Catholic conferences as the principle of culture, of freedom of progress – all that which differentiates it from the purely rationalist, revolutionary and abstract ideals of progress, and which misunderstands the conditions of the state of sin and the relativity of all natural law.

The concept of this Christian natural law does not belong only to Catholicism. As the Old Protestantism of both Confessions, Lutheranism and Calvinism, led to the idea of a unified Church and to the idea of a unitary churchly people's culture (*Volkskultur*) and Christian society, it had the need to compromise with the prevailing relations and the non-Christian ethical-legal orders (*außerchristlichen sittlich-rechtlichen Ordnungen*).[12] Exactly like Catholicism, Protestantism satisfied this need with the help of the Christian

---

11 'Punishment and remedy of sins'.

12 Troeltsch divided Church history into four periods: The 'early Church', 'medieval Catholicism', 'old Protestantism', and 'new Protestantism'. He specialized in the 'old Protestantism' of Luther and Calvin. See *Soziallehren*, *Kapitel* III, 2 and 3; and 'Luther, der Protestantismus und die moderne Welt' and 'Calvinismus und Luthertum –Ueberblick' in *Gesammelte Schriften IV*: 202–53 and 254–60.

concept of natural law, and these refined ideas are a power in our society today. Of course, the concept of natural law succumbed to certain modifications, and for both Confessions in very different ways.

Lutheran ethics differs from the Catholic above all in that it does not know the Catholic double morality, with its distinction between the lower masses of Christianity (*ermäßigten Massenchristlichkeit*) and the monkish elite. In the same way, Protestantism does not know the steps from nature to grace, from the natural forms of life (*Lebensformen*) to the Kingdom of Grace of the Church. The Protestant Church demands complete uniformity and principled equality of morality for all Christians under the release from exclusively individual and qualitative differences. It cannot order natural law and Christian law beside one another, but must draw them into each other. It must actualize Christian law immediately within and mediated by the natural laws of life (*naturrechtlichen Lebensformen*). It extracts this from its famous doctrine of vocational ethics (*Berufsittlichkeit*).[13] According to natural law, society disintegrates into the system of vocations and estates that it carefully supports in its differences, privileges and duties. The vocational action within this system of classification (*Ständesystem*) is now the contribution of the individual to the well-being and growth of the whole. It needs only a breath of inspiration from the sermon of words for this law of a natural vocational work distribution (*naturrechtlich-beruflichen Arbeitsgliederung*) for society to be freely convinced and to take it in. Christian brotherly love is completed here, especially in the ordered vocational work. The faithful vocational fulfilment is the way the family, state, society and economy can prove to the neighbour their God-filled love, the justification of the individual being in the holy community of God, as worked out through the relationship with the neighbour. For that, insofar as there are no non-compatible Christian spiritual vocations within this vocational system (*Berufssystem*), natural law excludes wholesale trade, speculation and credit economy, as well as all the social classifications of revolutionary spirit.

The natural law of the state of sin recognizes state, power, law, death penalty, personal property, trade and the like, only within the limits of reasonable purposefulness (*vernünftigen Zweckmäßigkeit*) for a peaceful, quiet God-blessed conduct of life. Therefore, everything depends on the notion that this natural law is fully conservative and maintains once and for always the given classification of a mutually supportive system of society. Lutheran natural law is, therefore, extremely conservative. This conservatism shows itself in particular ways: in order to secure equality and order, the law of power and

---

13 Both Lutherans and Calvinists emphasize the notion of *Beruf*, which can be translated as 'calling' or 'vocation'. Weber expends considerable effort in explaining the historical background and Luther's use of *Beruf* in the *Protestantische Ethik* (see Part I, section 3).

authority must be stressed to the highest level. This happens primarily so that natural law and its relativity and its conditionality through sin is stressed. Sins necessitate repression through force, and therefore natural law requires the most extreme deification of the ruling force (*herrschenden Gewalt*). The essence of force is power and blood-law, so it may use them against every revolution. Resistance against the ruling force (*herrschenden Gewalt*) would be conceptually absolutely contrary and, as a result, is not permitted – not just by Christian [doctrine] but also by natural law. The execution of hard force is, therefore, specifically a Christian calling [as well as] a Christian fulfilment of the demands of natural law with the spirit of brotherly love.

Obviously, under these circumstances it is natural that the vocation for natural law and the conduct of relationships demanded by the Christian conviction of love (*Liebesgesinnung*) occasionally clash hard with each other. The soldier and the hangman are not easily thought of as being executors of the Sermon on the Mount. Here, Luther teaches that a differentiation is imposed on us between the morality of office and vocation, the natural law of the state of sin and the inner, pure, personal Christianity of the radical conviction of love (*Liebesgesinnung*) that is demonstrated in the unofficial activities of our lives. The duality of relative natural law and true Christian morality is now instilled in the heart of each individual. The result of this is that Lutheran natural law has become a glorification of the dominating forces (*herrschenden Gewalten*) and a patriarchal submission in the system of classes and vocations. During this time, the true, inner Christianity of the heart (*Herzenchristlichkeit*) fundamentally has nothing at all to do with anything political and social and submits to them. Its forms manifest themselves according to the power of the conviction of love (*Liebesgesinnung*). That remains the essence of Lutheranism today: a radical, conservative, patriarchal natural law of the glorification of force (*Gewaltverherrlichung*) and an inner politico-social indifference towards true religious conviction. This appears under contemporary circumstances as the politico-social impotence of the Lutheran Church.

In Calvinism, the development of Christian natural law was entirely different and in many respects exactly the opposite. Indeed, at first, Calvin based everything on Lutheran suppositions and his feeling for authority was not much less than Luther's. Only Calvin believed from the beginning in a close melding of natural law and Christian demands. Insofar as he wanted to establish the ideal of a real Christian society in Genf, he believed that natural law more closely approximated the Christian ideal and that Christian demands more closely approximated natural law. The establishment of a Christian community (*Gemeinwesens*) required a reduction of strict Christian ideals and a stronger and immediate use of the forms of life (*Lebensformen*) of natural law. Here, both were brought substantially closer to each other. The expression of this and the means that enabled it to come about was the identification of Old Testament and New Testament morality. Calvin did not acknowledge the split between Christianity of the heart (*Herzenchristlichkeit*) and the official vocational morality that made Luther's societal ethic so idealistic, but also passive and indifferent. He wanted to establish a Christian society, and had therefore to give natural law a more direct and positive relationship in the creation of a Christian community (*Gemeinwesens*). Thus, he stressed the strengths of the rational, the critical and the positive increasing value of natural law, and deduced from this the right to resist a godless authority that appeared contrary to reason. Obviously, one should proceed in the most loyal way possible, and go with the failure of the lawful force to the revolutionary right only over the next subordinate official and possessor of power. Where these are not present or they deny you [your right], then logically nothing remains but the sovereignty of the people. Over this narrow bridge progressed the great French, Dutch, Scottish and English struggles of Calvinism up to the radical natural law of democracy, people's sovereignty and creation of rational society through the individual. Clearly, opinion was still that the aim of all revolution and rational societal ranking was to re-establish Christian rules to live by (*Lebensordnung*) and the dominance of authority.

In addition, Calvinistic natural law always retains from relative natural law the principle of the recognition of inequality, and from that the emerging gradations of the very unequal rights and obligations and, in particular, the emphasis of duties that natural and holy law impose on rights. In its entirety, however, it is a continual repressing of the relative tendencies of natural law and an increasing accentuation of the abstract and the absolute. Insofar as Anglo-Saxon Calvinism changed from the state-church system to the independent church system, it was suited to the formal arrangement of the Church leadership arising from a voluntary contract from the individual. In those countries since then, Calvinism goes with the liberal and democratic parties. The mainstays of the English liberals are the dissenters from the Calvinistic middle class. And in America, churchly individualism and the political are intimately connected by a complete external separation from institutions. Today, the Calvinists are the partisans of liberal demands, the supporters of the peace movement and the anti-slavery movement, the reformers of public life in the sense of a rational, purposeful natural law (*rationellen naturrechtlichen Zweckmäßigkeit*) and the participation of the individual in community activities.

Those are the developments of natural law in the great Church and Confessional domains. But natural law is not missing from the basis of the sects. The melding of Christian law and natural law became so accepted that the sects did not withdraw from this equation. And, even for the sects, this equation must also be an advantage, for the age-old and original conditional demands of nature and reason could also lay claim to Christ's law. However, the meaning and function of natural law as the basis of sects are entirely different from the natural law of the churches. Foremost for the churches was relative natural law considered with the state of sin, in order that the given political, social and economic orders could at the same time be recognized and regulated in accordance with a legal title (*Rechtstitel*). It is self-evident that the people's church and the state church (*Volks- und Landeskirchen*) are led by a church for universal culture. The matter is entirely different with the sects. The sects especially fight against the thoughts of churchly universal culture and mass Christianity and instead collect aroused and awakened Christians into voluntary communities (*Freiwilligkeitsgemeinden*). Thus, they have little to do with any compromise of relative natural law. They emphasize absolute natural law and its identity with the strict law of the love of Christ. Freedom, equality, communal property and the equal status of man and woman, as it was with Adam and Eve in the very beginning: this is the natural law of the sects that is demanded in the name of reason and as is demanded by Christian revelation.

Obviously, there needs to be a differentiation between a double direction within sect types. On the one hand there are suffering and patient sects and on the other, aggressive, reforming sects. The first is the norm but the other is certainly not very unusual. Above all, the sects are inclined to follow the principles of the Sermon on the Mount, in which it is demanded that one patiently endures the suffering and evil of the world and the oppression, persecution and malevolence, and renounces revenge in accordance with the word of God. It demands the complete separation of the religious community from the political, freedom of faith without any external pressure, but recusancy as a notional opposition in case of persecution, and seals its Christianity through martyrdom.

Under pressure from the world and without dominance and victory, Christian law is without universal and public validity. This is expected only with the 'end time', with Christ's return and with the establishment of the Thousand Year Kingdom (*tausendjährigen Reiches*). Thus, natural law and Christian law will triumph only in the 'end time'. For the present, Christians keep the law of revelation (*Offenbarungsgesetz*) among themselves with its limitations on the ways of living (*Lebensformen*, 'forms of life') of a suffering and oppressed sect. For the non-Christian world in the state and in society, the validity of relative natural law is not exactly denied and is even occasionally recognized. Christians also simply accept the suffering and enduring under alien ways of living (*Lebensformen*) and either completely or partially reject holding office or support for certain laws, war, the death penalty, certain oaths and the worldly conduct of life. Here, therefore, natural law has a positive significance only for the future; for the present it represents the equality, freedom and brotherliness that are found only in the relationships of community members with one another. In modern times, when the sects are less oppressed and persecuted, they manifest a strong elective affinity to the democratic and Christian-social parties.

The transformation from the suffering and enduring sects to the aggressive and reforming ones was made everywhere where the pressure of persecution or the enthusiasm of the passion regarding the coming of the Kingdom of God appeared to be close. That means that in the time of the impending return of Christ, the days of suffering and enduring are at an end and the time of the establishment of the Kingdom of God and of nature have arrived. This was the proclamation of Fra Dolcino's peasant group and the promise of the Joachim literature.[14] This was how the Hussites Laborites and the Munster Baptists, and a few groups of Independents reformed. They surrendered to radical democratic and socialist or even communist thinking. Such evangelical- and natural law-based thinking was also not far removed from the Peasant Wars, which were about natural law and the law of reason. Naturally, threads extend from here to modern socialism. Modern socialism is completely analogous on this score to Christianity; it rejects only the eschatological grounding and instead of a God, demands immediate transformation of the world, a manifestation of the holy progressive will (*göttlichen Fortschrittswillens*) and speaks of the great social movement of the time. But even the social democrat also had links to these powerful ideas (*Gedankenmächten*). The English revolution brought predecessors of socialism, and from Catholicism these thoughts are also contained in the ideas of Saint-Simon, which precede socialism. Contemporary Marxist socialism has clearly broken that inner connection with this absolute Christian natural law of freedom and love and instead of love, all is founded on class struggle; and instead of the holy word reigning through natural law, it is a matter of economic development.

The third type, mysticism, has the least to do with Christian natural law. It is the radical individualism, unfettered by organization, of the immediate

14 In the thirteenth century, Fra Dolcino led a group called the 'Brothers of the poor Life of Jesus', and they devoted themselves to the apostolic life and the ideal of poverty. This northern Italian group was at odds with the Church. The Joachimites followed Joachim von Floris, a twelfth-century southern Italian, who held many of the same beliefs as the 'Brothers'. He held that there were three ages: the Age of the Father, or the Law; of the Son, or the sacraments; and the Spirit, or freedom.

religious experience. Mysticism has no need to adapt to any particular organization and can dispense with those who have no interest in its essential purpose. Thus, the Church does not need to compromise with relative natural law nor, like the sect, does it need a perspective on the realization of absolute natural law or the law of revelation. It is essentially where they [the Churches are not], as often happens, bound up with the sects, and are indifferent to or put up with the natural formations as they are. However, in one aspect, this mysticism has an objective relevant significance for natural law, without, of course, using its name or introducing itself into this conceptual connection. A particular feature of consistent mysticism is that it views all historical, cultural and dogmatic procedures and rules that have continued into the present fundamentally and simply as the depositing of religious proceedings identical to those of today. Christianity is the effect of Christ in us, and Christ possesses holy principles. From this, the same principle is found in all the various forms of historical Christianity everywhere, with only relative external differences. Indeed, the deep piety of non-Christians builds upon this principle, and even heathens, while not recognizing Christ in us, base themselves on it. The inner light is therefore identical with the holy essence of reason (*göttlichen Vernunft-wesen*) of mankind everywhere [and is] identical with natural light. From this follow, as with the sects, demands for civil tolerance and for the non-interference of state force in religious struggles; and the cessation of struggles in the light of purely spiritual forces. Moreover, from this develops the idea of freedom of conscience as a demand for human beings, as a claim of all relative truth based upon life and self-presentation in which is also contained the core of truth (*Wahrheitskerns*). It is the relativism in the treatment of the different Confessions and the external religious forms or dogma as the relative expressions of a universal idea that lies behind all [religions]. It is the inner light, the inner word, or it is the expression of the sparks and suns of the Logos-Christ in every heart. This inner light and its manifestation in every human being is frequently posited in relation to natural ethical law and also embodies the core in all positive ethical and legal formations. Against this, the component of the ever ethical-legal natural law of this freedom of conscience is not, to my knowledge, indicated. It appears to me first as the influence of the Enlightenment theory of natural law, or a theory of human rights, which are construed as the legal consequences that flow from reason, if one includes this legal freedom of conscience within natural human rights. The issue stems from the circle of mysticism and the sects in the sense that they flowed together with mysticism.

Churchly natural law, on the contrary, exactly reversed the designation of the external unity of culture and religion as the demand of reason of natural law, as did Rousseau's sketch of human rights. The American Constitution was the first to offer the mystical idea of it in a rational and legal form. However, it is not to be overlooked that in Spinoza's *Theological-Political Tractatus*, the demands for scientific freedom (*wissenschaftlichen Denkfreiheit*) are connected with the mysticism of the inner words, the Christ in us, the natural light and the natural demand for tolerance connected with law, as it appeared that human rights were not written into the state contract. Spinoza did not live for years with the Rinjnsburger Collegium for nothing. However, he also necessarily held this modern, anarchistic ideal balanced with the idea of a cultural unity of state and Church (*staatlich-kirchlichen Kultureinheit*), and Hobbes also gave as the goal for philosophical sociology the new modern founding of the state.

With this we have passed over to the modern, classical natural rights of the eighteenth century, which signify the beginning of a new, modern conception of sociology, independent of the Church and religious standards, which not only dominates the instinctive self-perception of every community but also deeply permeates the legal and factual construction of all modern institutions. To replace the supernatural holy foundations and ties of the profane and churchly domains comes the ideal of a radical new construction of the unification of individuals. This opens up rational considerations of the purposes of the community for the individual and the desire to develop a legal theory from these fundamental ideas. By contrast with churchly culture and its relative natural law, and with the eschatological enthusiasm of the sects, there is, without doubt, something new.

Considering the previously presented connections from the beginning a strong continuity is apparent; the classical profane natural right is bound up with the Church, and the rise of modern, radical, social new forms are closely bound up with a transformation of the old Hellenistic-Christian ideas. In addition, profane natural law is an ideal legislation in a many-sided, almost utopian opposition between real natural laws and the nature of society. The new conception of the state rests on a strong religious faith in the purposeful nature of the world, in the triumph of the good and the reasonable and in an echo and a transformation of Christian-Judaeo-Stoic theism. The continuity between the culture of the Enlightenment and the culture of the Christian Church is considerably greater than the conceptual struggles of generations and the modern disinclination against the Church appear to be. The difference lies only in the optimism and the immediacy, and in the replacement of all supernatural revelation by the capacity for logical and explanatory reason and universal ethics, and from that, the unity and radicalism of the construction comes out of a single, dominating idea. Individualism is freed totally or partially, practically or only theoretically, from its patriarchal admixtures and holy sanctions into its emerging social forms. That is, in its effect, certainly something new. The old, treasured ideas are substantially and also partly conceptually, continued and transformed. The still unwritten history of liberalism and the natural law world view (*naturrechtlichen Weltanschauung*) should always take that into consideration. This is clearly not to deny that modern profane natural law has its determining influence and reasons. The urge of the citizens to emancipation, the rationalism of the absolutist state, the analogy of the universal rational-mathematical manner of thinking – all of this has its great significance. But these connections demand their own discussion. Here, only a suggestion of the impact of churchly natural law can be pointed out.

This connection is already recognized by the greatest thinkers of the modern world. Even Hobbes designated as an ideal the merging of Christian moral law with the constructed natural law, which he developed without any consideration of the state of sin and independent of the Stoic-Christian and the Epicurean ideal. However, the universal formulations of the problem, as he sees them, and, indeed, his entirely new construction, come from the churchly doctrine of natural law. Grotius, in his conscious appropriation of Stoic and Scholastic predecessors, expanded the area of validity of the absolute, pure, rational natural law and placed the Christian moral law in the position of the not-necessarily-reasonable advice and excesses, similar to those of Catholicism. It is entirely evident that Pufendorff embedded his new knowledge into the old. In his *Theological-Political Tractatus*, Spinoza called the law of his ethic 'natural law' and identified it with the law of Christ.[15] Locke constructed an ethical and legal natural law entirely freely from that and identified it with a new understanding of Christianity. Leibniz uses the title, *'le naturel'*, the concept of *Lex naturae*, for his ethics, and in his introduction to his *Codex diplomaticus juris gentium* he derives it from natural law, just like St Thomas. Christian Wolff, in his expansion of natural law, expressly retained its identity with Christian moral law. Everywhere in Voltaire is the concept of the *loi naturelle*, and Rousseau's glorification of nature rests on moral natural law. In the implementation of the jurists, natural law was a split into an abstract, purely conceptual and hypothetical, taking into consideration special circumstances and conserving in natural right the difference between an absolute and a relative natural law. Also unmistakable is how the radical, reformed development first gave support and impetus to the new theories, while the Lutheran and Catholic world followed only slowly. Not least is the emphasis and effectiveness of churchly natural law, which contained Stoic elements in

15 While Troeltsch does not indicate the title, it is clear that it is Spinoza's work that he has in mind.

an independent unfolding and, outside the church, could even be connected to the Roman legal tradition.

It is not possible here to go further. The investigation of these points has not progressed, as has the history of philosophy, with the illumination of the sociological component of philosophical thinking. However, the universal outlines of the connections are clearly drawn. And, of course, from this something else has become clear. Profane, modern, natural law is similar to the Christian and Stoic social ideal, is an ideal, a legislated idea, that relies from the beginning on the construction of the historical proceedings of the foundations of society, but it becomes ever more clear that it is in truth an idea and not a social natural law or a historic law. Rousseau and, above all, Kant, clearly expressed that any judgement of society is conditional (*Sollmaßstäben*, literally, 'under measurements of should') and there is no explanation of the real proceedings of its genesis. We look here at the clash of the idea with the natural laws of society, as was the case for Stoic-Christian natural law. The old Christian ideal arose in connection with the individualistic and pessimistic disintegration of ancient society, but soon enough reverted from the demands of nature. But, soon enough, it placed in opposition its other side; that is, the opposite for the demand for the replacement for the idea of an actually dominating nature. The ideal of modern natural law raised itself with the collapse of the old feudal ties and with the emancipation of the free powers of life, but it often also rashly opposed the real natural constitution of society. Modern thinking alone does not consider the sin of creating resistance, but of the difficulties that become apparent through the evolutionary, theoretical, racial, psychological and, finally, sociological natural laws. The profane modern natural law stands *mutatis mutandis* with liberal idealism and with the same struggles and difficulties once faced by the old Stoic-Christian idea.

Select Bibliography

This is necessarily a very selective bibliography. I have chosen only the most relevant primary works for inclusion. Regarding secondary works, those on Weber alone run into the thousands; those on Simmel and Troeltsch number in the hundreds. I have also included only a few of the many important and relevant German secondary works.

Primary Works

Georg Simmel

1892 *Die Probleme der Geschichtsphilosophie. Eine erkenntnistheoretische Studie.* Leipzig: Duncker & Humblot. Revised 1905.

1892–93 *Einleitung in die Moralwissenschaft. Eine Kritik der ethischen Grundbegriffe.* Stuttgart and Berlin: Cotta's Nachfolger.

1897 'Ferdinand Tönnies, Der Nietzsche-Kultus. Eine Kritik.' *Deutsche Litteraturzeitung.* 42.23: 1645–1651.

1900 *Philosophie des Geldes.* Berlin: Duncker & Humblot. *The Philosophy of Money.* Tr. Tom Bottomore and David Frisby. London: Routledge & Kegan Paul, 1982.

1904 *Kant. Sechzehn Vorlesungen gehalten an der Berliner Universität.* Leipzig: Duncker & Humblot.

1906 *Die Religion.* Frankfurt am Main: Rütten & Loening.

1907 *Schopenhauer und Nietzsche. Ein Vortragszyklus.* Leipzig: Duncker & Humblot.

1908 *Soziologie. Untersuchungen über die Formen der Vergesellschaftung.* Leipzig: Duncker & Humblot.

1911a *Hautprobleme der Philosophie.* Leipzig: G.J. Göschen'sche Verlagshandlung.

1911b *Philosophische Kultur: Gesammelte Essais.* Leipzig: Klinkhardt.

1918 *Lebensanschauungen. Vier metaphysische Kapitel.* Munich and Leipzig: Duncker & Humblot.

1984– *Simmel Gesamtausgabe.* Ed. Otthein Rammstedt. Frankfurt: Suhrkamp.
1990– *Simmel Studies* (formerly *Simmel Newsletter*). Editors-in-Chief: Klaus Letzel and Otthein Rammstedt. Bielefeld.
1992 *Soziologie. Untersuchungen über die Formen der Vergesellschaftung.* Ed. Otthein Rammstedt. Frankfurt: Suhrkamp. *Gesamtausgabe* 11.

Werner Sombart

1896 *Sozialismus und Sozial Bewegung. Nebst einen Anhang: Chronik der Sozialen Bewegung von 1750–1896.* Jena: Gustav Fischer.
— *Socialism and the Social Movement.* London: J.M. Dent & Company, 1909.
1902 *Der moderne Kapitalismus.* Leipzig: Duncker & Humblot.
1906 *Das Proletariat. Bilder und Studien.* Frankfurt am Main: Rütten & Loening.
1911 *Die Juden und das Wirtschaftsleben.* Leipzig: Duncker & Humblot.
— *Jews and Modern Capitalism.* Tr. M. Epstein. New Brunswick, NJ: 1982.
1913a *Krieg und Kapitalismus.* Munich and Leipzig: Duncker & Humblot.
1913b *Der Bourgeois. Zur Geistesgeschichte des modernen Wirtschaftsmenschen.* Munich and Leipzig: Duncker & Humblot.
1913c *Luxus und Kapitalismus.* Berlin: Duncker & Humblot. *Luxury and Capitalism.* Tr. W.R. Dittmar. Ann Arbor: University of Michigan Press, 1967.
1916–27 *Der moderne Kapitalismus. Historisch-systematisch Darstellung des gesamt-europäischen Wirtschaftslebens von seinen Anfängen bis zur Gegenwart.* Munich: Duncker & Humblot.
1919 *Grundlagen und Kritik des Sozialismus.* Berlin: Askanischer Verlag.
1923 'Die Anfänge der Soziologie', in Palyi: 3–19.
1937 *Die Zukunft des Kapitalismus.* Berlin: Buchholz & Weiswange.
1938 *Vom Menschen. Versuch einer geisteswissenschaftlichen Anthropologie.* Berlin: Buchholz.

Ferdinand Tönnies

1887 *Gemeinschaft und Gesellschaft. Abhandlung des Communismus und des Socialismus als empirischer Culturformen.* Leipzig: Fues.
— *Gemeinschaft und Gesellschaft. Grundbegriff der reinen Soziologie.* Darmstadt: Wissenschaftliche Buchgesellschaft, 1979.
— *Community and Society.* Ed. and tr. Charles Loomis. New York: Harper, 1963.
1892 'Friedrich Nietzsche. Also Sprach Zarathustra'. *Deutsche Litteraturzeitung* 50.10: 1612–1613.
1896 *Hobbes. Leben und Lehre.* Stuttgart: Fromman's Verlag.
1897 *Der Nietzsche-Kultus. Eine Kritik.* Leipzig: O.R. Reisland.
1907 *Die Entwicklung der sozialen Frage.* Leipzig: G. J. Göschen'sche Verlagshandlung.

1909 *Die Sitte*. Rütten & Loening. Frankfurt am Main.
1917a *Der englische Staat und der deutsche Staat. Eine Studie*. Verlag von Karl Curtius in Berlin.
1917b *Weltkrieg und Völkerrecht*. Berlin: G. Fischer Verlag.
1922a 'Ferdinand Tönnies', in *Die Philosophie der Gegenwart in Selbstdarstellungen*. Ed. Raymund Schmitt. Leipzig: Verlag von Felix Meiner: 1–35.
1922b *Kritik der öffentlichen Meinung*. Berlin: Springer Verlag.
1925–29 *Soziologische Studien und Kritiken*. Jena: G. Fischer.
1931 *Einführung in die Soziologie*. Stuttgart: Enke.
1935 *Geist der Neuzeit*. Leipzig: Hans Buske.
1998– *Ferdinand Tönnies Gesamtausgabe*, in Auftrag der Ferdinand-Tönnies-Gesellschaft. Ed. Lars Clausen, Alexander Deichsel, Cornelius Bickel et al. Berlin-New York: de Gruyter.
2001 *Community and Civil Society*. Ed. Jose Harris, tr. Jose Harris and Margaret Hollis. Cambridge: Cambridge University Press.

Ernst Troeltsch

1891 *Vernunft und Offenbarung bei Johann Gerhard und Melanchton. Untersuchung zur Geschichte der altprotestantischen Theologie*. Göttingen: Vandenhoeck & Ruprecht.
1902 *Die Absolutheit des Christentums und die Religionsgeschichte*. Tübingen: J.C.B. Mohr (Paul Siebeck).
— *The Absoluteness of Christianity and the History of Religions*. Louisville, KY: Westminster John Knox Press, 1971.
1904 'Das Historische in Kants Religionsphilosophie'. *Kant-Sudien*. 9.1 and 2.
1905 *Psychologie und Erkenntnistheorie in der Religionswissenschaft. Eine Untersuchung über die Bedeutung der Kantischen Religionslehre für die heutige Religionswissenschaft*. Tübingen: J.C.B. Mohr (Paul Siebeck).
1906a *Protestantisches Christentum und Kirche in der Neuzeit*, in *Die Kultur der Gegenwart. Ihre Entwicklung und ihre Ziele*. Ed. Paul Hinneberg. Berlin and Leipzig: Druck und Verlag von B.G. Teubner. 253–458.
1906b *Die Bedeutung des Protestantismus für die Entstehung der modernen Welt*. Munich and Berlin: Druck und Verlag von R. Oldenbourg.
1912 *Die Soziallehren der christlichen Kirchen und Gruppen*. Tübingen: J.C.B. Mohr (Paul Siebeck). (*Gesammelte Schriften 1*).
— *The Social Teaching of the Christian Churches*. Tr. Olive Wyon. Louisville, KY: Westminster John Knox Press, 1992 [1930].
1913 *Zur religiösen Lage, Religionsphilosophie und Ethik*. Tübingen: J.C.B. Mohr (Paul Siebeck). (*Gesammelte Schriften 2*).
1915 *Augustin, die christliche Antike und das Mittelalter*. Munich and Berlin: Druck und Verlag von R. Oldenbourg.
1922 *Der Historismus und seine Probleme. Erstes Buch: Das logische Problem der Geschichtsphilosophie*. Tübingen: J.C.B. Mohr (Paul Siebeck). (*Gesammelte Schriften 3*).
1924a *Der Historismus und seine Überwindung. Fünf Vorträge, eingeleitet von Friedrich von Hügel*. Berlin: Pan Verlag Rolf Heise.

1924b *Spektator-Briefe. Aufsätze über die deutsche Revolution und die Weltpolitik 1918/1922.* Mit einem Geleitwort von Friedrich Meinecke. Zusammengestellt und herausgegeben von H. Baron. Tübingen: J.C.B. Mohr (Paul Siebeck).

1925a *Aufsätze zur Geistesgeschichte und Religionssoziologie.* Ed. Hans Baron. Tübingen: J.C.B. Mohr (Paul Siebeck). (*Gesammelte Schriften 4*).

1925b *Deutscher Geist und Westeuropa. Gesammelte kulturphilosophische Aufsätze und Reden.* Ed. Hans Baron. J.C.B. Mohr (Paul Siebeck).

1925c *Glaubenslehre.* Ed. Gertrud von le Fort. Munich and Leipzig: Verlag von Duncker und Humblot.

1982– *Troeltsch-Studien.* Ed. Horst Renz und Friedrich Wilhelm Graf. Güterslohe: Gütersloher Verlagshaus Gerd Mohn.

1988– *Ernst Troeltsch. Kritische Gesamtausgabe.* Ed. Friedrich Wilhelm Graf, Volker Drehsen, Gangolf Hübinger, Trutz Rendtorff. Berlin: Walter de Gruyter.

Max Weber

1920 *Gesammelte Aufsätze zur Religionssoziologie.* Tübingen: J.C.B. Mohr (Paul Siebeck). Vols. 1–3.

1921 *Gesammelte Politische Schriften.* Munich: Drei Masken Verlag.

1922a *Gesammelte Aufsätze zur Wissenschaftslehre.* Ed. Marianne Weber. Tübingen: J.C.B. Mohr (Paul Siebeck).

1922b *Wirtschaft und Gesellschaft.* Tübingen: J.C.B. Mohr (Paul Siebeck).

— *Wirtschaft und Gesellschaft. Grundriss der Verstehenden Soziologie.* J.C.B. Mohr (Paul Siebeck).

— *Economy and Society. An Outline of Interpretive Sociology.* Ed. Guenther Roth and Claus Wittich. Berkeley: University of California Press. 1978 (1968).

1924a *Gesammelte Aufsätze zur Soziologie und Sozialpolitik.* Ed. Marianne Weber. Tübingen: J.C.B. Mohr (Paul Siebeck).

1924b *Gesammelte Aufsätze zur Sozial-und Wirtschaftsgeschichte.* Ed. Marianne Weber. Tübingen: J.C.B. Mohr (Paul Siebeck).

1946 *From Max Weber: Essays in Sociology.* Ed. and tr. H. H. Gerth and C. Wright Mills. Oxford: Oxford University Press.

1949 *The Methodology of the Social Sciences.* Tr. E. Shils and H. Finch. New York: The Free Press.

1958 *The Protestant Ethic and the Spirit of Capitalism.* Tr. Talcott Parsons. New York: Scribner's.

1984– *Max Weber Gesamtausgabe.* Ed. Horst Baier, M. Rainer Lepsius, Wolfgang J. Mommsen, Wolfgang Schluchter, Johannes Winckelmann. Tübingen: J.C.B. Mohr (Paul Siebeck).

1992 *Wissenschaft als Beruf/Politik als Beruf.* Ed. Wolfgang J. Mommsen and Wolfgang Schluchter in Zusammenarbeit mit Birgitt Morgenbrod. Tübingen: J.C.B. Mohr (Paul Siebeck). *MWG I/ 17*.

1994a *Max Weber. Briefe 1909–1910.* Ed. M. Rainer Lepsius and Wolfgang J. Mommsen in Zusammenarbeit mit Birgit Rudhard und Manfred Schön. Tübingen: J.C.B. Mohr (Paul Siebeck). *Max Weber Gesamtausgabe* II/6.

1994b *Max Weber. The Political Writings.* Ed. Peter Lassman and Ronald Speirs. Cambridge: Cambridge University Press.

1998 *Max Weber. Briefe 1911–1912.* Ed. M. Rainer Lepsius and Wolfgang J. Mommsen in Zusammenarbeit mit Birgit Rudhard und Manfred Schön. Tübingen: J.C.B. Mohr (Paul Siebeck). *Max Weber Gesamtausgabe* II/7.

(2001–) *Max Weber Studies.* Ed. Sam Whimster and David Chalcraft. London: Continuum Publishing.

2003 *Max Weber. Briefe 1913–1914.* Ed. M. Rainer Lepsius und Wolfgang J. Mommsen in Zusammenarbeit mit Birgit Rudhard und Manfred Schön. Tübingen: J.C.B. Mohr (Paul Siebeck). *Max Weber Gesamtausgabe* II/8.

Secondary Works

Adair-Toteff, Christopher (1994), 'Kant's Philosophical Influence on Classical German Sociology: Simmel's *"Exkurs über das Problem: Wie ist Gesellschaft möglich?"'*, *Simmel Newsletter* (now *Simmel Studies*), 4.1: 3–8.

Adair-Toteff, Christopher (1995), 'Ferdinand Tönnies: Utopian Visionary?', *Sociological Theory*, 13.1: 58–65.

Adair-Toteff, Christopher (2004), 'Neo-Kantianism', in Baldwin: 27–42, 815–17.

Adair-Toteff, Christopher (2005), 'Ernst Troeltsch and the Philosophical History of Natural Law', *The British Journal for the History of Philosophy*, 13.4: 733–44.

Baldwin, Thomas (ed.) (2004), *The Cambridge History of Philosophy 1870–1945.* Cambridge: Cambridge University Press.

Berman, Harold J. and Charles J. Reid, Jr. (2000), 'Max Weber as Legal Historian', in Turner: 223–39.

Bruun, H. H. (1972), *Science, Values and Politics in Max Weber's Methodology.* Copenhagen: Munksgaard.

Cahnman, Werner J. (ed.) (1973), *Ferdinand Tönnies: A New Evaluation.* Leiden: Brill.

Cahnman, Werner J. (1995), *Weber & Toennies: Comparative Sociology in Historical Perspective.* New Brunswick, NJ: Transaction Publishers.

Chapman, Mark (2002), *Ernst Troeltsch and Liberal Theology. Religion and Cultural Synthesis in Wilhelmine Germany.* Oxford: Oxford University Press.

Coakley, Sarah (1995), *Christ Without Absolutes. A Study of the Christology of Ernst Troeltsch.* Oxford: Clarendon Press.

Drescher, Hans-Georg (1993), *Ernst Troeltsch. His Life and Work.* Tr. John Bowden. Minneapolis: Augsburg Fortress Publishers.

Geiger, Theodor (1931), 'Soziologie', in Vierkandt: 568–78.

Hawthorne, Geoffrey (2004), 'Sociology and the Idea of Social Science', in Baldwin: 245–52.

Hennis, Wilhelm (1987), *Max Weber: Essays in Reconstruction.* Tr. Keith Tribe. London: Allen & Unwin.

Grundmann, Reiner and Nico Stehr (2001), 'Why is Werner Sombart Not Part of the Core of Classical Sociology? From Fame to (Near) Oblivion', *Journal of Classical Sociology*, 1.2: 257–87.

Featherstone, Mike (1991), 'Georg Simmel: An Introduction', in Simmel: 1–16.

Fogt, Helmut (1981), 'Max Weber und die deutsche Soziologie der Weimarer Republik: Außenseiter oder Gründervater?', in Lepsius: 245–72.

Frisby, David (1991), 'Bibliographical Note on Simmel's Works in Translation', in Simmel: 235–41.

Jaspers, Karl (1932), *Max Weber. Deutsches Wesen im politischen Denken, im Forschen und Philosophieren*. Oldenburg i. O.: Gerhard Stalling.

Jung, Werner (1990), *Georg Simmel. Zur Einführung*. Hamburg: Junius.

Käsler, Dirk (1981), 'Der Streit um die Bestimmung der Soziologie auf den Deutschen Soziologentagen 1910–1930', in Lepsius: 199–244.

Käsler, Dirk (1984), *Die frühe deutsche Soziologie 1909 bis 1934 und ihre Entstehungs-Milieus. Eine wissenschaftssoziologische Untersuchung*. Opladen: Westdeutscher Verlag.

Käsler, Dirk (1988) *Max Weber. An Introduction to His Life*. Tr. Patricia Hurd. Chicago: University of Chicago Press.

Kantorowicz, Hermann (1923), 'Der Aufbau der Soziologie', in Palyi: 73–96.

Lepsius, M. Rainer, (1981), 'Die sozialwissenschaftliche Emigration und ihre Folgen', in *Soziologie in Deutschland und Österreich 1918–1945*. Ed. M. Rainer Lepsius. Opladen: Westdeutscher Verlag.

Liebersohn, Harry (1988), *Fate and Utopia in German Sociology 1870–1923*. Cambridge, MA: MIT Press.

Lukacs, Georg (1918), 'Georg Simmel', in Simmel: 145–50.

Mayer, Jacob Peter (1956), *Max Weber and German Politics. A Study in Political Sociology*, 2nd edn. (revised and enlarged). London: Faber & Faber.

Mitzman, Arthur (1973), *Sociology and Estrangement. Three Sociologists in Imperial Germany*. New York: Knopf.

Mommsen, Wolfgang J. (1984), *Max Weber and German Politics 1890–1920*. Tr. Michael S. Steinberg. Chicago: University of Chicago Press.

Mommsen, Wolfgang J. and Jürgen Osterhammel (eds.) (1987), *Max Weber and his Contemporaries*. London: Unwin Hyman.

Palyi, Melchior (ed.) (1923), *Erinnerungsgabe für Max Weber*. Munich and Leipzig: Duncker & Humblot.

Ringer, Fritz (1969), *The Decline of the German Mandarins. The German Academic Community 1890–1933*. Cambridge, MA: Harvard University Press.

Rickert, Heinrich (1899), *Kulturwissenschaft und Naturwissenschaft. Ein Vortrag*. Tübingen: J.C.B. Mohr (Paul Siebeck).

Rickert, Heinrich (1902), *Die Grenzen der naturwissenschaftlichen Begriffsbildung. Eine logische Einleitung in die historischen Wissenschaften*. Tübingen: J.C.B. Mohr (Paul Siebeck). First half 1896; second half 1902; complete edition 1902.

Rubanowice, Robert J. (1983), *Crisis in Consciousness. The Thought of Ernst Troeltsch*. Tallahassee, FL: University Press of Florida.

Scaff, Lawrence (1989), *Fleeing the Iron Cage. Culture, Politics, and Modernity in the Thought of Max Weber*. Berkeley, CA: University of California Press.

Schiele, Friedrich (1909–13), *Die Religion in Geschichte und Gegenwart*.

Handwörterbuch in gemeinverständlicher Darstellung. Unter Mitwirkung von Herman Gunkel und Otto Scheel. Tübingen: J.C.B. Mohr (Paul Siebeck). Vols. 1–5.

Schluchter, Wolfgang (1981), *The Rise of Western Rationalism: Max Weber's Developmental History.* Tr. Guenther Roth. Berkeley, CA: University of California Press.

Schluchter, Wolfgang (1989), *Rationalism, Religion, and Domination: A Weberian Perspective.* Tr. Neil Solomon. Berkeley, CA: University of California Press.

Schluchter, Wolfgang (1996), *Paradoxes of Modernity: Culture and Conduct in the Theory of Max Weber.* Tr. Neil Solomon. Stanford, CA: Stanford University Press.

Schroeter, Gerd (1993), 'Book Reviews of C. Bickel and K. Herberle', *Journal of the History of the Behavorial Sciences,* 29: 59–63.

Schulze-Gaevernitz, Gerhart von (1923), 'Max Weber als Nationalökonom und Politiker', in Palyi: x–xxii

Sica, Alan (1988), *Weber, Irrationality and Social Order.* Berkeley, CA: University of California Press.

Simmel, Georg (1991), *Theory, Culture & Society. A Special Issue on Georg Simmel* 8.3, August.

Turner, Stephen and Regis Factor (1984), *Max Weber and the Dispute over Reason and Value. A Study of Philosophy, Ethics and Politics.* London: Routledge & Kegan Paul.

Turner, Stephen and Regis Factor (1994), *Max Weber. The Lawyer as Social Thinker.* London: Routledge.

Turner, Stephen (ed.) (2000), *The Cambridge Companion to Weber.* Cambridge: Cambridge University Press.

Verhandlungen der Deutschen Soziologentage (VDG, 1911). Tübingen: J.C.B. Mohr (Paul Siebeck).

Verhandlungen des Zweiten Deutschen Soziologentages (VDG, 1913). Tübingen: J.C.B. Mohr (Paul Siebeck).

Verhandlungen des Dritten Deutschen Soziologentages (VDG, 1923). Tübingen: J.C.B. Mohr (Paul Siebeck).

Verhandlungen des Vierten Deutschen Soziologentages (VDG, 1925). Tübingen: J.C.B. Mohr (Paul Siebeck).

Verhandlungen des Fünften Deutschen Soziologentages (VDG, 1927). Tübingen: J.C.B. Mohr (Paul Siebeck).

Verhandlungen des Sechsten Deutschen Soziologentages (VDG, 1929). Tübingen: J.C.B. Mohr (Paul Siebeck).

Verhandlungen des Siebenten Deutschen Soziologentages (VDG, 1931). Tübingen: J.C.B. Mohr (Paul Siebeck).

Vierkandt, Alfred (ed.) (1931), *Handwörterbuch der Soziologie.* Stuttgart: Ferdinand Enke Verlag.

Von Wiese, Leopold (1926), *Soziologie. Geschichte und Hauptprobleme.* Berlin and Leipzig: Walter de Gruyter.

Weber, Alfred (1931), 'Kultursoziologie', in Vierkandt: 284–94.

Weber, Marianne (1926), *Max Weber. Ein Lebensbild.* Tübingen: J.C.B. Mohr (Paul Siebeck).

Weingarten, Rudolph H. (1960), *Experience and Culture. The Philosophy of Georg Simmel*. Middletown, CT: Wesleyan University Press.

Willey, Thomas E. (1978), *Back to Kant. The Revival of Kantianism in German Social and Historical Thought, 1860–1914*. Detroit: Wayne State University Press.

Index

Catholic 13, 18, 26, 37, 83, 121, 122, 123, 130
Catholicism 25, 26, 114, 115, 122, 127, 130
causality 2, 7, 17
Cham 119
charm 52, 53, 54, 56
Chicago 1, 10
China 104
Christ 113, 114, 116, 117, 126, 127, 128, 129, 130
Christian/Christians 3, 13, 24, 25, 26, 38, 110, 113–27, 128, 129, 130, 131
Christianity 12, 13, 25, 112, 116, 119, 120, 122-28, 130
church 13, 25, 26, 38, 46, 49, 61, 62, 85, 86, 96, 98, 99, 115, 125, 126, 131
    Catholic 13, 37
    Christian 3, 13, 122, 129
    Early 13
    Lutheran 124
    state 125, 126
civitas dei 33
Cohen, Hermann 2, 8
community 24, 46, 61, 64, 70, 85, 89, 113, 115, 116, 117, 118, 119, 120, 123–27, 129
Comte, August 1, 14, 18, 19, 37, 61, 63, 67
concepts 3, 6, 11, 19, 22, 27, 39, 32, 33, 34, 45, 46, 58, 59, 62, 63, 65, 67, 70, 74, 90, 94, 95, 104, 118, 120, 121, 122, 123, 130
conference ix, xv, 14, 16, 17, 19, 23, 26, 27, 30, 31, 32, 35, 36, 37, 38, 39, 40, 41, 94
conflict 4, 17, 29, 33, 87, 113, 120
consciousness 33, 54, 55, 66, 67
constitution 75, 96, 128
conversation 53, 54
Coakley, Sarah 136
Corinth 100
Couleur 86, 76
Court society 55
courtoisie 51

Croce, Benedetto 3
Crusades 23
culture 2, 3, 22, 23, 27, 32, 33, 34, 35, 45, 52, 60, 64, 66, 67, 68, 69, 89, 94-100, 102-109, 111, 112, 115, 116, 117, 120, 121, 122, 126, 128, 129

Delbrück, Hans 15
Descartes, René 37
Deutsche Gesellschaft für Soziologie (D.G.S.) ix, xvi, 1, 15, 16, 17, 20, 21, 31, 32, 35, 38, 39, 40, 41, 43
Dilthey, Wilhelm 10, 13, 28
discipline ix, 57, 59, 70, 114, 120, 121, 122
dogma 13, 25, 114, 116, 128
dominance 72, 87, 88, 113, 118, 119, 125, 126
Dreyfus affair 80
drive 33, 46, 49, 50
Durkheim, Emile 1, 6
    Les Règles de la Methode Sociologique 1
Dutch 125

economics xviii, 29, 33, 59, 63, 68, 70, 76, 95, 98, 101, 104, 105, 106, 107, 123
economy xviii, 29, 33, 59, 63, 68, 70, 76, 95, 98, 101, 104, 105, 106, 107, 123
Ehrlich, Paul 99
empiricism x, 105
England 78, 81, 82
Erfurt 10
Ermsleben 8
erotic 46, 52, 88
essence xiii, 4, 17, 20, 21, 22, 24, 29, 45, 46, 47, 49–57, 60, 64, 66, 68, 70, 71, 74, 85, 88, 101, 110, 113, 115, 116, 121, 124, 128
Euclidean geometry 2
Eulenburg, Franz 16, 31, 91
Eve 126
experience 2, 3, 49, 52, 53, 56, 62, 64, 90, 106, 116, 128